Timber

Timber

A Photographic History
of Mississippi Forestry

James E. Fickle

Mississippi Forestry Foundation, Incorporated
University Press of Mississippi / Jackson

www.upress.state.ms.us

The University Press of Mississippi is a member of the Association of American
University Presses.

Frontis: Photograph of Sidney Streater for *American Lumberman,* courtesy of
Forest History Society

12 11 10 09 08 07 06 05 04   4 3 2 1

Library of Congress Cataloging-in-Publication Data
Fickle, James E.
   Timber : a photographic history of Mississippi forestry / James E.
   Fickle
      p. cm.
   Includes index.
   ISBN 1-57806-710-3 (alk. paper)
   1. Forests and forestry—Mississippi—History. 2.
Logging—Mississippi—History. 3. Forest products
industry—Mississippi—History. I. Title.
    SD144.M7F54 2004
    634.9'09762'022—dc22   2004008141

British Library Cataloging-in-Publication Data
available

Jacket and book design: David Alcorn, Alcorn Publication Design

For my late buddies Ferd Spangler, the king of the hanging lob, and Denny Hays, the master of the defensive overhead. The games are not the same without you.

Preface

This collection of images documents the history of the forests in Mississippi from the prehistoric era to the present. It is meant to stand on its own as a visual record, but it can also be viewed as a complement or supplement to my earlier book, *Mississippi Forests and Forestry*, which was published in 2001 by the University Press of Mississippi. It is my intention that the images in this volume will tell the story of how those forests have been experienced, used, abused, and restored by humans over some four hundred years of the historic era and countless earlier eons before people began to keep written records. The illustrations are not necessarily chosen because of their artistic merit—in other words, whether they are good, bad, or indifferent—but rather because they reflect one or another aspect of the story which needs to be told. I wrote the text, determined the matters that I wanted to illustrate, and then chose from the available images that told that story. Of course, when there were several options available I tried to select the photograph or other item that was most aesthetically pleasing or that presented the subject matter most clearly. I also tried to choose illustrations that showed areas or topics that may have been slighted in my earlier book. Historians make choices regarding whatever accounts they write, and it is doubtful that any two would tell the same story exactly the same way or include and exclude the same topics. They are also limited by the sources available to them during the time that they research. I hope that this book will address some of the gaps in my earlier work.

Most of the images are from Mississippi, but in a few cases I included photographs of or from nearby states when they illustrated a point that I wanted to make. While each state had its own peculiarities and characteristics, there was a great deal of similarity in the lumber regions of the South. They had much in common visually and in other ways as well. There are multiple photographs in many areas where people simply have an innate interest in the subjects; these include railroads and locomotives, sawmills, workers, lumber towns and camps, work animals, and prominent individuals. There are undoubtedly many other images in all of these areas that should have been included if they had been available or if I had known about them.

In a number of cases I started with photographs scanned from existing publications and was then fortunate to find the original prints. Often the process and results were fascinating. For example, I was able to scan a number of photographs of the Lamb-Fish Lumber Company's hardwood operations in Charleston, Mississippi, from a company publication printed for the 1915 Panama Pacific Exposition in San Francisco. The publication is rare, and I was thrilled to find an original copy which I could scan. Some of those scans are in this book. However, at the same time I was scanning these photos I looked at a collection of Memphis lumber industry photos in the Memphis Room of the Memphis Public Library, and immediately realized that most of them were the same photos! They were done by a talented pioneer Memphis professional photographer,

Clifford H. Poland, and had been mislabeled as Memphis photographs simply because the photographer was a Memphian. I was excited about now having a number of these original images, which also appear in this book. Similarly, I was able to use several original photographs by the New Orleans photographer John N. Teunisson, whose work and subjects are much like Poland's.

One of the gratifying aspects of the research was the generosity and assistance of other scholars. There are a few photographs in this book of the Foster Creek Lumber Company of Stephenson, Mississippi, a company which Dr. Gilbert H. Hoffman and his colleagues Tony Howe and David Price will fully examine in their forthcoming book on the subject. Charles A. Heavrin of Memphis shared his knowledge of the Anderson-Tully Lumber Company, a hardwood firm which had mills in Memphis and Vicksburg, as well as a fleet of Mississippi River watercraft. Charlie pointed me toward current Anderson-Tully president Charles R. Dickinson, Jr., for originals of the photographs in Charlie's book on Anderson-Tully, and Chip Dickinson and his staff went beyond the call of duty by providing originals of the Heavrin photographs, including some that had to be retrieved from frames hanging in the company's offices!

I have provided only a brief narrative as an overview accompanying the images in this volume. There is enough text with each to put the image in perspective. Although the illustration comments are not footnoted, in many cases the material came from the archives or published source in which the photograph was found. On most topics there are much fuller discussions and evaluations available in *Mississippi Forests and Forestry*. That work is also thoroughly documented, so the reader can refer to it for information concerning both primary and secondary sources, libraries, and archives that contain materials that will allow deeper immersion in the subject. Some of the photographs in this volume have been reproduced from other works. These images are in most cases unavailable other than by computer scanning, and for others the costs of photographic prints from the institutions where they are housed are prohibitive for a volume of this size. I am appreciative of the authors who first found or used them and to the publishers that made them available in their earlier forms. In some cases the same photographs are in several collections, and the ultimate ownership is uncertain. If there are mistakes in identification or description on some of the photographs, I look forward to hearing about them so that they can be corrected in future editions.

Historians can learn much from photographs—in some cases more than they can from many oral histories or written records. The ways in which people are posed by a photographer, the subjects chosen for documentation, how human beings arrange themselves and relate to other people or items in a picture often reflect much about an era, a society, an institution, a group, or an individual. They can thus be viewed and enjoyed on many different levels. It is my hope that the images in this volume will provide a number of satisfactions for its readers, on many levels, and that with its companion volume it will serve as a comprehensive record of the forests of Mississippi and the people whose lives they have affected.

Acknowledgments

The number of people who generously shared their time, interest, and expertise as I worked on this book is unusually large. First and foremost were the members of my family, who were often assaulted by my excitement and enthusiasm as I found wonderful photographs, often in unexpected places. Inalee Woods in particular never seemed bored as I rhapsodized over old pictures dealing with a subject and a part of the country which were not her own. On one occasion a family member accused me of being on an "ego trip" when I returned from a week's research in Mississippi and loudly proclaimed that "this is going to be a great book!" In fact, as I tried to explain, I was convinced that it was going to be a good book not because of me, but because of the exceptional quality and abundance of the original photographs that I had been lucky enough to find and that others had found for me. In any case Inalee, Jeanne, Valerie, Steven, Ashley, Cyndi, Angie, Shan, Terri, April, Kenny, Kelsey, Billy, Matthew, and Bryce all contributed to the creation of a positive working environment. My friends Wayne, Waymon, Denny, and my coffee pals, particularly Billy, provided support, encouragement, and an occasionally needed respite.

Those who helped and encouraged me include Mississippians who are almost too numerous to mention. As I traveled the state visiting individuals, archives, and other institutions, I was repeatedly impressed by the interest and pride that Mississippians have in their history and their desire to have that history available to a wider audience. They were unfailingly helpful, kind, and considerate as I looked for historic images, and were also genuinely interested in insuring that the picture was complete—not some edited, sanitized version that would be stripped of its reality. In some cases my search seemed like that of a detective trying to find a missing person, and their help was invaluable. For example, I needed pictures of two individuals who were extremely important in the story of professional forestry in the state, and who despite their prominence were strangely undocumented in most visual collections. One was Posey Howell, perhaps the most famous early forester in the state, and the other was Mrs. G. H. Reeves, a Jackson clubwoman who was instrumental in achieving the creation of the Mississippi Forestry Commission, and who then served on the commission and was later employed by the agency. Given the prominence of these individuals I thought their pictures would be readily available, but I found quite the opposite to be true. In the case of Howell, I got significant help from Dr. Charles Sullivan of the Mississippi Gulf Coast Community College at Perkinston, who actually furnished a picture of Howell. Ironically—for months I had found nothing—shortly thereafter John Guthrie of Wiggins supplied some additional Howell photographs. John and his wife have been stalwart supporters of this project. In the meantime I was having a similar lack of success in the case of Mrs. Reeves. The Mississippi Department of Archives and History and the archives of Mississippi State University and the University of Southern Mississippi turned up nothing, nor was there anything in the photo files of the Jackson

Clarion-Ledger. I called upon Anne Guidry, editor of the Mississippi Forestry Association's magazine, *Tree Talk*, for assistance, and her efforts led me to Mrs. Tommie Rosenbaum, president of the Mississippi Federation of Women's Clubs. An associate of Mrs. Rosenbaum's searched the federation's files and found nothing, but Mrs. Rosenbaum later suggested that I send an inquiry to the *Clarion-Ledger*'s column "Ask Jack Sunn." Mr. Monte Williams wrote an "Ask Jack Sunn" column describing my search, and within a few days I got a message from Ms. Rachel T. Rowley that led me to Mrs. Reeves's daughter, Mrs. Roger I. Martin, Jr., of Purvis, who sent me both a picture and an article with information about her mother. In a final note of irony, it turned out that Mrs. Reeves's sister was married to Posey Howell! Kindnesses, coincidences, and ironies were abundant in the preparation of this book.

I hardly know where to begin in acknowledging those who were so helpful at the University of Memphis. I received the strong support of history department chair Dr. F. Jack Hurley and the valuable assistance of Ed Franks and Jim Cole of the Mississippi Valley Collection in the McWherter Library. My colleagues Dr. Jonathan Judaken, Dr. Daniel Unowsky, Dr. D'Ann Penner, Dr. Dennis Laumann, Dr. Charles Crawford, and Dr. James Blythe were generous in their support of and interest in a project that was light years away from their own fields of specialization. They helped to create a wonderful working atmosphere. The office staff of the history department, Ann Rand, Jena Murakowski, and Karen Bradley, were both cheerful and helpful, and never complained about the ridiculous copying and xeroxing schedule I foisted upon them during the course of this project. Dr. Thad Wasklewicz, director of the Memphis Center for Advance Spatial Analysis in the Department of Earth Sciences, Geography Program, at the University of Memphis, kindly took time out of his extremely busy schedule to assist me. Patricia LaPoint of the Memphis Room at the Memphis Public Library went out of her way to be helpful.

Dr. Theodor Leininger of the Center for Bottomland Hardwoods Research at Stoneville went above and beyond the call of duty in providing materials that I needed, as did his colleagues Dr. Nathan Schiff, Charles "Bo" Sloan, and Dr. Brian Roy Lockhart, who supplied photographs and valuable information about pondberries, bears, and cypress. Bo, who directed the Louisiana black bear restoration project in Mississippi, provided particularly interesting information about a bear that Valerie, Steven, and Kelsey encountered near Grenada on the way to a signing ceremony for my last book at the state capitol in Jackson.

Michael Hennen of the Mississippi Department of Archives and History and his colleagues Clinton I. Bagley, Jeffrey S. Rogers, and Elaine Owens were extremely helpful, as were Sam Brooks, Forrest Cooper, and Melvin Butler of the United States Forest Service's Mississippi headquarters in Jackson. Art Nelson, an old friend and colleague, offered sound advice and provided some wonderful photographs. I should also note that the caption material for some of the photographs is based on information in published sources where I originally found them. I want to thank Dr. Gilbert H. Hoffman of Hattiesburg, who, with his wife, Kalani, kindly entertained me in their home during a research trip to Hattiesburg. Dr. Hoffman and his colleagues Tony Howe and David Price are currently working on a history of the Foster Creek Lumber Company of Stephenson, Mississippi, which will be welcomed by students of Mississippi's forests and railroads. Dr. Hoffman has placed a wonderful collection of photographs of sawmills, towns, equipment, and people in the archives at the University of Southern Mississippi. He maintains control over the collection and unfortunately decided not to allow its use for this volume. However, the photographs constitute a valuable resource that I hope will be accessible to other scholars in the future. The staff of the USM archives, Dr. Patterson Toby Graham, Kalani Hoffman, and Yvonne Arnold, were extremely helpful in providing access to other collections and copies of the images I selected. Stewart and Lynn Crosby Gammill of Hattiesburg also generously opened their home to me, and allowed me to examine the wonderful photographs and other materials in their collection. Beyond that, they took the time to copy materials that I selected for inclusion in this book.

They also provided a copy of "B. Forest Rover, Sawmill Foreman" by G. Louis Isbell, which is quoted below in a description of the sawmilling process. The Gamills' copy was furnished by Benjamin McClelland Stevens, Jr. Words cannot repay my debt to the Gammills.

Charles Bates, assistant curator in charge of the Railroad Collection of the Allen County Historical Society in Lima, Ohio, was very helpful in providing information about that institution's enormous collection of photographs documenting the history of the Shay locomotive. Robert F. Brzuszek and Tammy F. Schock of the Crosby Arboretum at Picayune contributed both interest and materials, as did Linda A. Tufaro, director of the Pearl River County Library System in Picayune. Joseph S. Weston and the Weston family kindly supplied photographs of the important Weston operations at Logtown and of family leaders. Harold Gordon of Louisville, Mississippi, kindly supplied a magazine with pictures of logging with mules. General John S. Napier was generous in sharing the results of research for his excellent book on the lower Pearl River region, and Charles A. Heavron, Charles R. (Chip) Dickinson, Jr., and Chip's administrative assistant, Yvonne Ritter, led me to original photographs of the Anderson-Tully operations around Vicksburg. Sally Spier Stassi and Pamela D. Arceneaux of the Williams Research Center in New Orleans assisted me in finding some of the final pieces of the puzzle, and, as with previous projects, I am again indebted to Cheryl Oakes of the Forest History Society, Sandy Hayes and Donna Smith of the Lauren Rogers Museum of Art in Laurel, and Mattie Sink of the Department of Archives at Mississippi State University for their professionalism, expertise, and assistance. Jennifer Aronson of the archives at the University of Mississippi provided assistance, as did Rachel Galen of the Forest History Archives at Stephen F. Austin State University. James D. Elledge of Hattiesburg supplied a family photograph of the Mississippi Forestry Commission inspecting the reforestation work at Bogalusa, Louisiana, in 1928. Andy Fobes of the Mississippi Port Authority at Gulfport worked to track down historic photographs of lumber exports.

John Simley of Home Depot helped me locate a visual of "green certification," and Gina M. Amster and Teresa Dombach of the Home Channel News kindly supplied a photograph and helpful information. Tommy Miller was tireless in his support of the project and furnished photographs that were needed in several areas, and Donald S. Bell of Bruce, Mississippi, went far beyond the call of duty to uncover an original copy of a booklet that I badly needed, supplied photographs and information, and generally made it his mission to be sure that his part of the state was properly represented in this book. The many photographs of north Mississippi and of hardwood operations are a testimony to his support and persistence. The booklet, on the Lamb-Fish Lumber Company, was kindly provided by Mrs. Harold Breedlove of Charleston, Mississippi. It is especially valuable because the names of many workers in the photographs are penciled in. Steve Butler helped to put me in touch with valuable sources, and Steve Corbett provided some timely research and lobbying on my behalf. Bruce Alt of the Mississippi Forestry Association was quite willing to help whenever I called on him. Bill Colvin shared his vast experience and expertise in suggesting where I might find photographs, and Mississippi State Forester James L. Sledge, Jr., was unfailingly generous and helpful. Polly Anderson of Calhoun, Louisiana, who was the first female forestry graduate of Mississippi State University, kindly supplied a photograph.

Maria L. Schleidt, archaeologist at the Laurel office of the United States Forest Service, is doing a wonderful job of collecting the history and artifacts of the area. She went far beyond the call of duty in making the Civilian Conservation Corps photographs she had collected available to me, and her colleagues, district ranger Robert E. Lee, forestry technician Jeff Cotter, planning forester Andy Barwick, and fire management officer Harvey R. Moody, all contributed to a very productive trip to Laurel. Ms. Schleidt's work on the activities of the Civilian Conservation Corps in the Chickasawhay Ranger District will soon lead to a scholarly article on the subject. A former CCC corpsman still living in the area, Lewis H. Bailey, generously let me use his treasured personal photographs of the period.

Victoria Mocsary and Lois Wagner of the Center for Southeast Louisiana Studies at

Southeastern Louisiana University were very helpful in locating some of the wonderful A. L. Blush photographs of the piney woods that are in their collection. Professor Charles A. Gresham of the Belle W. Baruch Institute of Coastal Ecology and Forest Science at Clemson University and Bill Rousseau and Mike Schaefer of the Silvatech Corporation in Bethel, Vermont, helped me locate and acquire illustrations of the latest developments in sawmill technology.

Craig Gill and Anne Stascavage of the University Press of Mississippi contributed valuable assistance on both this book and its predecessor. Craig was influential in making final cuts in the photographs and determining the final shape of the volume. Carol Cox showed genuine interest in the subject and did a wonderful job of editing the copy. I appreciate the work done by Cliff Prince and Shane Gong to bring the project to fruition. John Langston and David Alcorn are responsible for its final design and appearance. The staff at the University Press of Mississippi are real professionals, and their collective enthusiasm and talents contributed significantly to whatever merits this book may have.

To all of the folks listed above, and to those who were inadvertently omitted, I extend my heartfelt gratitude and appreciation.

Introduction

The period of time before humans kept written records is called prehistory. In prehistoric times Mississippi was inhabited by various Native American groups who utilized the forests in a variety of ways—for hunting, for agriculture, for ceremonial purposes, for defense. They altered the forest landscape in many ways, especially by burning.

The Mississippi forests encountered by the first European explorers were not "virgin," if virgin means forests unaltered by human activity. They were vast, and included various types of trees, including the pines which are found in many parts of the state, hardwoods, and extensive stands of cottonwoods along the rivers. As Europeans began to settle in Mississippi, they, too, used wood from the forests in many ways—for housing, for fencing, for furniture and tools, and to make boats, wagons, and other conveyances. Water-powered sawmills, producing lumber primarily for local use, began to appear along various waterways, being concentrated particularly in the south. Some areas were extensively logged, particularly along navigable rivers where "wood hawks" harvested and sold logs as fuel for steamboats plying the waters.

Most early Mississippians were farmers, and much of the forest was cleared for agricultural use. Areas were cut. Vast acreages were burned. Logrollings became a familiar part of the pioneer farmers' culture. Forests and trees were sometimes seen as impediments standing in the way of development, or "progress." These patterns persisted to some degree well into the middle of the nineteenth century.

The commercial potential of the forests was not generally recognized until the development of national markets for lumber as the nation urbanized and industrialized during the second half of the nineteenth century. The ravenous appetite for lumber led to the rapid depletion of the forests of New England and the Great Lakes states. Only then did the large-scale commercial lumbermen begin to look toward the vast forests of the South and of Mississippi. Even then, Mississippi's forests could not really be exploited without efficient transportation to get the logs to the mills and lumber from the mills to markets. The construction of an extensive railroad network in Mississippi during the second half of the nineteenth century represented the last piece of the puzzle.

The commercial lumbering that came to Mississippi in the late nineteenth century was dominated by breakthroughs in technology and by the dictates of finance.

The technology of late nineteenth-century lumbering centered around the use of the steam engine. Steam locomotives pulled log cars into the forest via narrow-gauge tracks. After the trees were felled and delimbed, the logs were pulled to the trackside by enormous steam-powered skidders and lifted onto the cars with loaders which were also propelled by steam. Enormous steam-powered mills then processed the logs and produced the lumber, which was shipped out by railroad to markets around the South and in other parts of the nation. Chicago was a major northern market for Mississippi lumber. Lumber exports became important, and ports like Pascagoula were heavily dependent on the lumber export trade. Mills of all sizes, hardwood and softwood, were located in various parts of the state. Some were tiny, portable "peckerwood" mills; others were enormous operations featuring the latest technology. The crews that labored in the woods and in the mills consisted of both blacks and whites, and the camps and towns in which they lived were rigidly segregated by race.

Nineteenth-century lumbering was a migratory industry. Many of the lumbermen came from outside Mississippi and especially from the depleted lumber regions of the North. The large operations ran on borrowed money, often in the form of timber bonds, which were sold with the forests as collateral. Interest rates were high, and both the lumbermen and their lenders felt obliged to harvest as much timber as they could as rapidly as possible. These pressures produced the prevailing philosophy of "cut out and get out" lumbering, in which the operators cut as rapidly as possible and then moved their operations to new locations when the woods were cut over.

The cutover lands were left in devastated condition, and many logging camps and mill villages became virtual ghost towns. Some camp houses and other structures were simply loaded onto railroad cars and carried to the next location. Despite the fact that a few lonely voices were beginning to question these procedures, little or no thought was given to selective cutting or reforestation.

There were exceptions. Some of the lumber giants were native Mississippians, or families who chose to stay, and who attempted to manage their lands responsibly and operate on a continuous and permanent basis. Production peaked in the early twentieth century, and many of the large mills closed and lumbermen migrated from Mississippi. Most of the remaining operations were small "peckerwood" mills utilizing smaller trees and patches of forest that their larger brethren had found too insignificant to work.

During the late 1920s and much of the 1930s most people gave up on the Mississippi lumber industry as dead, and thought that the magnificent forests that had once covered a large percentage of the state were gone forever, replaced by an unending cycle of poverty and marginal agriculture. President Franklin Delano Roosevelt referred to the South as the nation's number-one economic problem, and travelers crossing Mississippi traversed a barren landscape of denuded and eroded lands, pockmarked by huge gullies and ravines and scarred by recurring wildfires, many set by woods arsonists.

Ironically, just as things seemed at their worst, forces were emerging that would trigger an amazing recovery and restoration of both Mississippi's forests and her forest products industry. First was the dawning realization that there were still many small mills producing a significant volume of lumber from Mississippi's supposedly barren woodlands. Second was the fact that a new crop of trees, the "second forest," was emerging on lands that had been neither seeded nor planted, and natural regeneration from seed trees was producing what some considered a miracle on Mississippi's cutover lands. Third was the scientific research being done by people like chemist Charles Holmes Herty that made it possible to utilize southern pine, Mississippi's most prevalent species, for the production of wood pulp. This breakthrough opened the door for the rise of the pulp and paper industry in Mississippi, an industry which made use of smaller timber than the lumber manufacturers did and which, because of large investments and fixed costs, could not easily move from place to place, thus making it imperative that the forest lands be managed so that they would remain perpetually productive and able to supply enormous paper mills. Also, in Laurel, William T. Mason undertook the research that produced Masonite, and the Masonite Corporation became a major Mississippi industry. Fourth was the emergence of a new class of professionally trained foresters and vocal citizen activists who insisted that forests should be responsibly managed. Most believed in a forest management philosophy built around Gifford Pinchot's famous definition of conservation as "wise use." Most of the foresters were graduates of the nation's developing system of forestry schools at the university level, and while many worked for government agencies, a growing number were industrial foresters, working for responsibly managed lumber and paper companies. The major problems and tasks confronting these pioneer foresters were controlling fire, excluding hogs and other pests, establishing boundary lines, introducing programs of selective cutting, implementing planting and seeding programs, and undertaking campaigns of community relations.

Also during the 1930s the federal government became far more deeply involved in forest reclamation and management in Mississippi. During the years of the Great Depression five national forests were established in the state, and the federal government initiated the massive Yazoo–Little Tallahatchie Flood Control project in north Mississippi. They also began extensive research on the cultivation and use of hardwoods at the Southern Hardwoods Laboratory at Stoneville. By the time of World War II, Mississippi's forests had recovered to the point of being major suppliers of lumber and other material for the mobilization effort.

During the postwar years the pent-up demand for housing brought on by wartime controls created a feverish market for lumber, with a great deal of poorly manufactured material going out and to some extent damaging Mississippi's reputation for lumber quality. However, the industry attempted to regulate and enforce standards through its own organizations, such as the Southern Pine Association, and both the quality and reputation rebounded. By this time the "second forest" was everywhere to be seen, and lumber companies which had left the state, like the Edward Hines Company, returned to harvest the recovered forests. Also, the pulp and paper industry now moved into Mississippi in a major way. New high-speed lumber mills, massive paper manufacturing plants, new woods technologies, large log concentration yards, and massive chip mills began to appear across the state. Semitrucks replaced railroad spurs, and tree-length logging became a major activity. New forest products empires emerged, like the one built by Warren A. Hood.

By the time Mississippi entered the late twentieth century, her forests had recovered to the point that forested acreage equaled (some said exceeded) the amount encountered by the first European explorers at the beginning of the historic era. The third forest was being harvested, and the fourth forest was springing from the ground. The forest products industry had again become a central pillar of the Mississippi economy in terms of the number of manufacturing establishments, revenue generated, and employment. But there were new concerns and controversies. Old style "conservationists" were supplanted by a new breed of "environmentalists" who questioned many of the practices of the forest products industry, with much of their attention focused on clear-cutting, chip mills, the proliferation of even-aged pine plantations, and the protection of endangered species, such as the red-cockaded woodpecker and dusky gopher tortoise. Some questioned the training and values of professional foresters, believing that they were too "commodity" oriented. It was charged that the national forests, including those in Mississippi, were little more than timber farms for the forest products industry. Industry itself began to change. "Green certification" of forest products and woods management in accordance with the standards of the Sustainable Forestry Initiative now became the order of the day. As Mississippi entered the new century there was a massive wave of industry mergers, acquisitions, and reorganizations that created the specter of an uncertain future. Mississippi now confronted an age in which the forests had recovered, the public was demanding a greater voice in the management of both public and private lands, and the structure of industry control and management was unclear.

Timber

Old-growth longleaf pine forest.

When the first Europeans came to Mississippi, they encountered large and luxuriant forests of enormous longleaf pines in the southern part of the region.

In other areas, there were forests of mixed hardwoods.

The forests had been altered by pre-historic Native Americans who used fire for ceremonial purposes, for hunting, and for clearing the land for farming.

Hardwood forest.

A forest cleared by burning.

Scene in a longleaf forest.

Early settlers commented on the park-
like appearance of the longleaf forests. Some said that the atmosphere was
like that of a cathedral.

Despite their majesty, the forests
were regarded by many early settlers as
impediments or obstacles to be removed,
or "conquered," as they "civilized" the region and cleared the land for cultivation.

One of the first commercial uses of the forest was the production of fuel for steamboats on the Mississippi River and other navigable waterways. The forests in these areas were stripped by "woodhawks" who sold fuel to the passing vessels.

Farmers sometimes operated small sawmills to produce lumber for their own use and to sell locally. Some small operators specialized in sawmilling. Their mills were hand powered, or utilized water or animals for propulsion.

Frontiersmen using girdling and fire to clear the forest for farming.

Steamboat wooding at night.

Primitive pit-sawing operation.

With the perfection of the steam engine, steam power soon was used in most mills of any size. The first steam-powered sawmill in the region appeared in nearby New Orleans in the early nineteenth century. Most early sawmills utilized a primitive sash saw with an up-and-down motion.

Early sash saw.

Photograph of cypress brake.

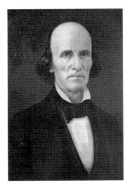

Portrait of Andrew Brown.

Portrait of Henry Weston.

As sawmilling grew, cypress logs from the Yazoo-Mississippi River delta were rafted downriver to mills in Vicksburg, Natchez, and New Orleans.

One of the most important of the early Mississippi lumbermen was Andrew Brown, a Scottish immigrant who established a mill at Natchez in 1828. Another early Mississippi lumberman was Henry Weston, who came to New Orleans from Maine in 1846 and soon moved to Pearlington, Mississippi.

The Mississippi was the oldest locomotive used on a Mississippi logging railroad, reputedly having been built in 1834 in England. The engine was used on the Meridian, Brookhaven, and Natchez line from about 1880 until 1891. The photograph was taken in 1893.

In the period following the Civil War, the depletion of forests in the Great Lakes states and the construction of railroads in the South combined with other factors to attract large lumber manufacturers to Mississippi.

Spur lines were extended into the woods to transport logs from the forests to the mills.

Workers from the Gilchrist-Fordney Lumber Company constructing a logging spur. Note the unhewn round crossties.

S ome spur lines were so primitive that the trains ran on wooden poles rather than steel rails.

The Cole pole road locomotive, invented by Captain W. E. Cole of Montgomery County, Alabama, had grooved wheels that ran on round poles instead of steel rails and cut the cost of building a logging spur.

Track-building or steel crew in 1920. The photograph is by John N. Teunisson, a commercial photographer in New Orleans who recorded scenes of logging and sawmilling in south Mississippi. His work parallels that of Memphis photographer Clifford H. Poland, who produced similar images in north Mississippi during the same period.

Many logging trams were pulled by side-geared Shay locomotives, which were excellent at negotiating tight turns. Others used traditional-type locomotives. The logging roads commonly had narrow-gauge tracks.

Gilchrist-Fordney Lumber Company track-laying crew.

Eastman-Gardiner Lumber Company Shay locomotive with Barnhart loader.

Gilchrist-Fordney Lumber Company Engine 202 with loader.

Eastman-Gardiner Lumber Company camp scene with Shay locomotives in about 1895.

Two locomotives and log trains.

Two locomotives under steam in the woods was a photographer's dream, as were long trains of log cars.

Gilchrist-Fordney Lumber Company log train in the woods.

Eighty-five-ton Heisler locomotive of the Foster Creek Lumber Company pulling a log train.

Two Gilchrist-Fordney Lumber Company log trains in the woods.

This photograph of a Sumter Lumber Company log train was inherited by Arthur M. Nelson, Jr., when his company, Flintkote, took over Sumter's lands in east Mississippi. It hung in Art's train room for over fifty years.

Mules being used to cross-load logs.

Mules, horses, or oxen were some-times used in the cross-loading of logs onto trains.

Logs were often dragged through the woods to the logging spurs on "big wheels" or "caralogs" with slip tongues. The wheels were as large as eight feet in diameter, and the carts were commonly pulled by mules or oxen.

Another method of moving logs in the southern woods was the eight-wheel Lindsey Log Wagon, invented and manufactured in Laurel. The wagons were easily copied by other manufacturers.

"Big Wheels in Mississippi." From a lantern slide. Loaded cart pulled by mules.

A Lindsey Lumber Company wagon. Dr. S. W. Lindsey is shown with his foot on the front truck tire, and Mr. Sam Lindsey, Sr., is at the back of the truck cab with his foot on the running board.

PRICE LIST AND SPECIFICATIONS

OF THE

LINDSEY

EIGHT-WHEEL LOG WAGON

THE LINDSEY REDUCES YOUR
LOGGING COST 40 PER CENT

Manufactured Only by the

LINDSEY WAGON COMPANY

LAUREL, MISSISSIPPI

Advertising brochure for the Lindsey Log Wagon.

Eastman-Gardiner Lumber Company ox lot.

Lindsey Log Wagon pulled by oxen.

Lamb-Fish Lumber Company workers with axes accompany a loaded log wagon. This is the first of several photographs in this book by the Memphis photographer Clifford H. Poland, whose work was similar to that of his New Orleans counterpart, John N. Teunisson.

Log wagon and horses belonging to the Foster Creek Lumber Company.

Lamb-Fish Lumber Company crew using oxen to cross-load an eight-wheeled wagon.

A Lamb-Fish Lumber Company woods scene showing oxen pulling an eight-wheeled log wagon.

Solid-wheeled wagons were used to haul logs through muddy areas, and were sometimes pulled by crawler tractors. The wheels were not actually solid, but were "boxed" by boards nailed across them to keep out mud so that they would turn more easily.

Cross-loading logs onto a railroad car.

Oxen skidding log.

Oxen, mules, horses, and, later, crawler tractors were used to skid logs in the woods. Logs were also moved by two-wheeled carts called "bummers."

Mules skidding logs in woods.

Logging equipment and mules belonging to Percy Bowman in the Caledonia, Mississippi, vicinity.

Although the older methods of skidding, loading, and hauling logs with mules, horses, and oxen continued in use, the age of steam brought giant steam-powered skidders and loaders to the woods. The steam skidders dragged logs attached to cables through the woods to the tramways and did incalculable damage as the logs uprooted the young growth in their path and gouged the ground. After a log had been skidded to trackside for loading, a worker who was called a rehaul man and who was usually on mule or horseback took the cable and tongs back into the harvested area for attachment lumber to another log. The Memphis photographer Clifton H. Poland often took pictures in the woods or mills and would later attach signage to the photos so that equipment manufacturers could use them in advertisements.

Crawler tractor skidding logs in a muddy area of north Mississippi.

McGiffert loader from the Marathon Lumber Company.

Gilchrist-Fordney Lumber Company skidder and crew.

Lamb-Fish Lumber Company Lidgerwood skidder with rehaul men on mules ready to take the cable and tongs back into the cutover area. A copy of this photograph without the signage is in the Memphis Room of the Memphis Public Library.

Lamb-Fish Lumber Company workers have attached tongs on a log so that it can be pulled in by the skidder. A copy of this photograph with signage is in the Memphis Room of the Memphis Public Library.

Double-end Clyde rehaul skidder from the Foster Creek Lumber Company.

Eastman-Gardiner Lumber Company skidder and crew.

Lamb-Fish Lumber Company log loader and crew. Another copy of this photograph with signage is in the Memphis Room of the Memphis Public Library.

American Log Loader in operation. This loader ran along railroad rails bolted to the top of each car being loaded.

Eastman Gardiner Lumber Company Barnhart loader on crib trestle.

American Log Loader belonging to the H. Weston Lumber Company loading cars in a virgin pine area which had been clear-cut. This machine could load sixty cars of logs daily.

Gilchrist-Fordney Lumber Company skidder and crew.

Steam skidder in operation.

Lamb-Fish Lumber Company log train with skidder barely
visible in background.

Goodyear Yellow Pine
Company steam skidder
and logs in about 1920.

Goodyear Yellow Pine Company skidding and loading logs
in about 1920.

Lamb-Fish Lumber Company hardwood logs along a logging
spur in north Mississippi.

Gilchrist-Fordney Lumber Company log dump.

Unloading logs from a truck to a train near Knoxville,
Mississippi, in 1937.

Logs were also moved by water, although not to the extent seen in the northern woods.

Unloading logs from train into mill pond.

Steamboat loading logs at Carthage, Mississippi, in 1853.

The Anderson-Tully Lumber Company steamboat *Dan Quinn* pushing a barge loaded with logs.

Loading pulpwood on a barge wharf near Vancleave, Mississippi, in 1939.

Unloading logs from a barge at Anderson-Tully Lumber Company mill in Vicksburg.

Moving logs by barge on the Pearl River to the H. Weston Lumber Company mill at Logtown.

Technological changes in the woods were paralleled by developments in the sawmills. Saw filers were among the most highly skilled sawmill workers. While mills cutting pine were clearly the most important, Mississippi also had a significant hardwood industry located mostly in the northern part of the state. Some of the following photographs are by the Memphis photographer Clifford H. Poland, taken at the Lamb-Fish Lumber Company, which produced hardwood lumber at Charleston. As noted earlier, Poland took some of his photographs into the studio and added advertising signage promoting equipment manufacturers, and both versions of many are in the collections in the Memphis Room at the Memphis Public Library. I have included several with the signage in order to make the machinery more understandable to readers who are unfamiliar with the technology of sawmills.

There are many published and unpublished descriptions of the sawmilling process, but one of the best is in a story by the fictitious sawmill foreman B. Forest Rover, who is a creation of G. Louis Isbell: "I'll try to give you a off-handed description of the Spike Knott mill. First off, the log pond with the mill a-settin' about twenty feet back from it, the engine room jam up against the mill and the boiler room on the far side of the engine room. Then the 'bull chain' running in a trough, with one end under water in the pond and a slantin' up to the log deck inside the mill, about fifteen feet above ground. The log is floated into the bull chain trough and cleats on the chain grabs it and hauls it to the log deck, where it is kicked out by a steam piston and rolls down the sloping log deck to the carriage. The 'carriage' runs on a track and carries the log back and forth against the saw. It is worked up and down the track by the 'shot-gun feed.' This is just a big steam cylinder and piston, like them on a locomotive, but the piston is fastened to the carriage and has a stroke of forty feet instead of four. The log is handled and turned on the carriage by . . . a big steel bar with teeth in it to

and everything that goes through them goes into the 'slab-conveyor' which takes it to the boiler room for fuel. The lumber, after going past the trimmer saws, is the yard foreman's worry."

Rufus F. Learned, Andrew Brown's stepson, is credited with introducing the band saw to Mississippi.

catch the log. It works up through the log deck out of another steam cylinder. The carriage . . . is controlled by the sawyer with levers that connect to the steam valves on the cylinders. This is a very delicate-like operation, but with powerful results. To move the lumber after it is sawed off the log, there is rollers driven by a belt and shaft, called the 'live rolls.' The lumber goes on the live rolls to the edge where the bark is sawed off the edges and then the lumber drops on some moving chains which take it under the trimmer saws, where it is trimmed up and cut to the best length. The slabs and edgings go on another set of moving chains to the 'slasher-saws.' The slashers are all on one shaft and four feet apart

A high-speed circular cutoff saw.

Band saw head rig.

Logs entering the Eastman-Gardiner Lumber Company mill
on the jackslip or "bull chain."

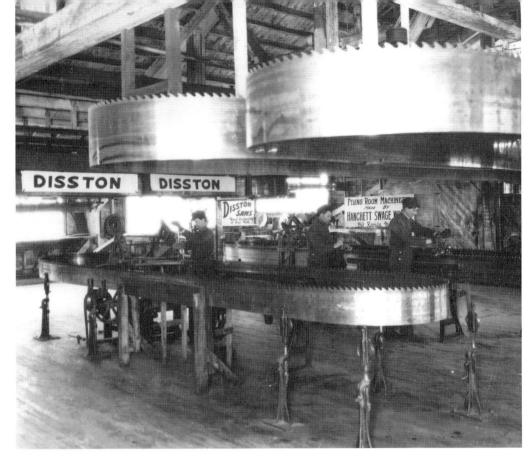

Saw-filing room and filers of the Lamb-Fish Lumber Company at Charleston, Mississippi.

Lamb-Fish Lumber Company band saw.

Band saw and carriage at Anderson-Tully Lumber Company.

Nine-foot Prescott bandmill at Anderson-Tully Lumber Company during the 1920s.

Electrically powered planing mill at the Sumter Lumber Company in Electric Mills, Mississippi.

Edging lumber at the Charleston, Mississippi, mill of the
Lamb-Fish Lumber Company.

As the Mississippi lumber industry rose to national prominence, its leaders included both native southerners and immigrants from the North. Some of the northerners were lumbermen who came south as the forests of their own regions were cut over.

Trimmer saws, which trim the lumber into commercial lengths. These were part of the Lamb-Fish Lumber Company's operation.

Grading and sorting green lumber at the Lamb-Fish Lumber Company mill.

Edward Hines of Chicago
owned Mississippi's Hines
Lumber Company. The
Hines Lumber Company cut
out in Mississippi, moved to
the Pacific Northwest, and
later returned to the Mag-
nolia State to harvest timber
and manufacture lumber
from the restored "second
forest."

Native Mississippian
L. O. Crosby created several
Mississippi lumber firms,
stuck it out during the
tough times of the 1920s
and 1930s, and attempted
to implement reforestation.

Philip S. Gardiner led the
Eastman-Gardiner Lumber
Company of Laurel and was
president of the Southern
Pine Association in 1921.

Brothers F. (Frank) L. Fair, Claude Fair, and D. L. Fair, Sr.,
led the D. L. Fair Lumber Company of Louisville, Mississippi.

E. L. Bruce, who lived in
Memphis, founded the
hardwood firm E. L. Bruce
and Company and the town
of Bruce, Mississippi.

Another Memphian was
Christopher J. Tully, who
migrated from Michigan to
become one of the founders
of the Anderson-Tully Lumber Company with mills in
Memphis and Vicksburg.

Frank W. Gilchrist of
Laurel's Gilchrist-Fordney
Lumber Company, which
cut out in 1937 and moved
to Oregon.

During the glory days of the late
nineteenth and early twentieth
centuries, Mississippi had some of the
nation's largest and most modern sawmills, as well as many smaller operations.

One problem for lumber industry historians was the frequency of mill-complex
fires that often destroyed company
records.

R. F. Learned and Son Lumber Company hardwood sawmill at Natchez. The mill was located "under the hill" on the banks of the Mississippi River. Photograph taken in about 1920.

The Sumter Lumber Company mill at Electric Mills had a daily capacity of three hundred thousand feet and was one of the first electrically powered operations in the South.

The L. N. Dantzler Lumber Company mill at Moss Point.

Major-Sowers Sawmill Company mill at Hattiesburg, Mississippi.

Crosby Lumber Company sawmill at Crosby, Mississippi, in June 1939. This operation was originally called the Foster Creek Lumber Company, and the town was named Stephenson. After the Crosby interests bought it in the early 1930s, both the company and the town were renamed.

Old hardwood sawmill of E. L. Bruce and Company at Bruce, Mississippi, in 2002.

Eastman-Gardiner Lumber Company sawmill #2 at Laurel,
Mississippi.

H. Weston Lumber Company sawmill and other buildings at
Logtown, Mississippi, on the lower Pearl River. The mill
could produce nearly six million board feet annually.

Gilchrist-Fordney Lumber Company sawmill and pond at
Laurel, Mississippi.

Postcard view of the J. J. White Lumber Company mill at
McComb, Mississippi.

Long-Bell Lumber Company mill at Quitman, Mississippi.

The Rosa Lumber Company mill at Picayune, Mississippi, produced millions of board feet annually. This photograph shows the lumber-sorting racks.

The Rosa Lumber Company mill pond in about 1918.

The Goodyear Yellow Pine Company mill at Picayune, Mississippi, in the early 1900s.

Anderson-Tully Lumber Company hardwood sawmill on the harbor at Vicksburg, Mississippi.

The J. J. Newman Lumber Company mill at Sumrall.

Postcard view of the Jordan River Lumber Company's Kiln, Mississippi, sawmill.

Life in the Mississippi lumber industry revolved around the mill towns and logging camps. The mill towns were sometimes owned by the companies, and some featured housing, retail, educational, medical, and recreational facilities that were superior to those in nearby traditional communities. The logging camps were company owned and were fairly primitive. The camps were moved as the companies cut their way through Mississippi's forests. Living arrangements in the towns and camps were segregated, with separate quarters for whites, African Americans, and foreigners. Some companies allowed the loggers' families to live in the camps; others did not. The YMCA had a presence in many of the towns and camps, providing recreation, shower facilities, and religious activities in buildings furnished by the companies.

Company houses in Electric Mills, Mississippi, home of the Sumter Lumber Company, in 1924. The company was proud of the cement walks and screened porches on the residences.

African American section of Stephenson.

Street scene in a Long-Bell Lumber Company town.

Street scene in the white section of the Foster Creek Lumber
Company mill town of Stephenson.

Lamb-Fish Golf Association.

The Lamb-Fish Golf Association, Charleston, Mississippi.

Lamb-Fish Athletic Club—Base Ball Park.   Lamb-Fish Athletic Club—Base Ball Team.

The Lamb-Fish Athletic Club baseball park and baseball team.

Store in Camp Allen, the Gilchrist-Fordney Lumber Company camp thirteen miles north of Laurel in Jasper County, Mississippi.

Boarding cars and logging camp office of the Sumter Lumber Company.

Logging camp office of the Foster Creek Lumber
Company.

General view of the Foster Creek Lumber Company's logging
camp. The large building in the background on the left is the
camp store.

Interior scene in Foster Creek logging camp hotel.

Commissary cars in Eastman-Gardiner Lumber Company
logging camp.

Interior of Eastman-Gardiner Lumber Company's "The Red Store" in 1896.

Interior view of the Stephenson store.

Another view of the Stephenson store interior.

Hospital in Electric Mills, Mississippi, home of the Sumter
Lumber Company.

MOVING DAY, WISNER, MISS.

Moving day at Eastman-Gardiner Lumber Company's
logging camp at Wisner, Mississippi.

Logging camp of H. Weston Lumber Company located
about five miles southeast of the logging headquarters at
Westonia, Mississippi, in 1910.

Portable house at Eastman-Gardiner Lumber Company's
Cohay Camp with Barnhart loader.

Tent camp of a hardwood logging operation in the Mississippi
Delta. Probably run by the Lamb-Fish Lumber Company.

View of Gilchrist-Fordney Lumber Company houses in Camp
Allen. Built in 1930 for about thirty thousand dollars, the
camp had thirty houses for whites and twenty for African
Americans, all with electric lights and water.

Partial view of portable logging camp in Jones County, Mississippi, taken in about 1925.

The Pine Grove Inn in the Goodyear Yellow Pine Company's Camp Anderson, which was located about twelve miles northwest of Picayune.

Another view of portable housing in Camp Anderson. Note the wheels under the housing.

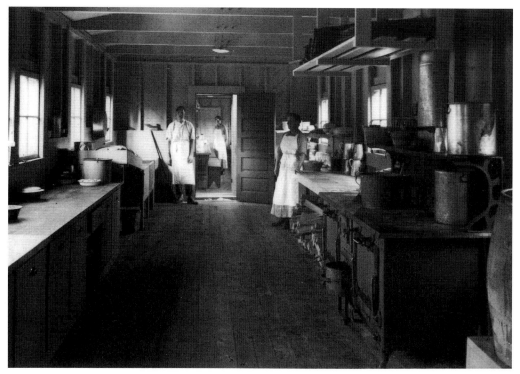

Railroad logging camp kitchen of Sumter Lumber Company.

Kitchen in logging camp hotel of the Foster Creek Lumber Company.

Kitchen in Eastman-Gardiner Lumber Company logging camp.

School in Foster Creek Lumber Company logging camp.

School car in Eastman-Gardiner Lumber Company logging camp.

School for African Americans at Stephenson, Mississippi.

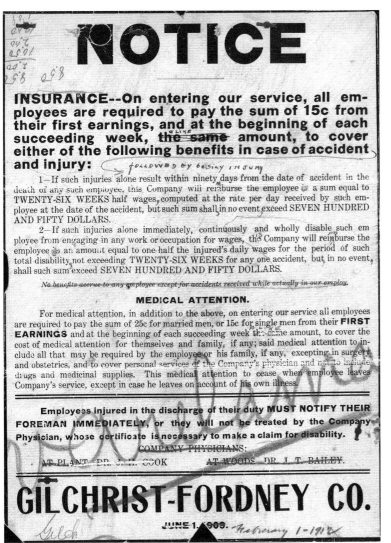

NOTICE

INSURANCE--On entering our service, all employees are required to pay the sum of 15c from their first earnings, and at the beginning of each succeeding week, the same amount, to cover either of the following benefits in case of accident and injury: *followed by bodily injury*

1—If such injuries alone result within ninety days from the date of accident in the death of any such employee, this Company will reimburse the employee a sum equal to TWENTY-SIX WEEKS half wages, computed at the rate per day received by such employee at the date of the accident, but such sum shall in no event exceed SEVEN HUNDRED AND FIFTY DOLLARS.

2—If such injuries alone immediately, continuously and wholly disable such employee from engaging in any work or occupation for wages, the Company will reimburse the employee an amount equal to one-half the injured's daily wages for the period of such total disability not exceeding TWENTY-SIX WEEKS for any one accident, but in no event, shall such sum exceed SEVEN HUNDRED AND FIFTY DOLLARS.

No benefits accrue to any employee except for accidents received while actually in our employ.

MEDICAL ATTENTION.

For medical attention, in addition to the above, on entering our service all employees are required to pay the sum of 25c for married men, or 15c for single men from their **FIRST EARNINGS** and at the beginning of each succeeding week the same amount, to cover the cost of medical attention for themselves and family, if any; said medical attention to include all that may be required by the employee or his family, if any, excepting in surgery and obstetrics, and to cover personal services of the Company's physician and not to include drugs and medicinal supplies. This medical attention to cease when employee leaves Company's service, except in case he leaves on account of his own illness.

Employees injured in the discharge of their duty MUST NOTIFY THEIR FOREMAN IMMEDIATELY, or they will not be treated by the Company Physician, whose certificate is necessary to make a claim for disability.

COMPANY PHYSICIANS:

AT PLANT—DR. J. H. COOK   AT WOODS—DR. J. T. BAILEY.

GILCHRIST-FORDNEY CO.

JUNE 1, 1909. *February 1-1916*

Gilchrist-Fordney Lumber Company broadside stating company medical and accident compensation policies in June 1909.

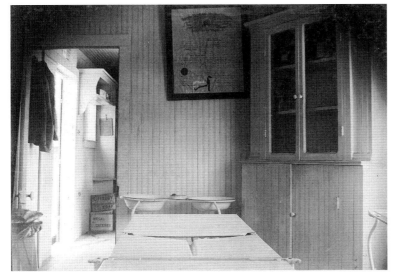

Operating room in drugstore car at Eastman-Gardiner Lumber Company logging camp.

Workers in the Mississippi lumber industry during the "cut out and get out" era of the late nineteenth and early twentieth centuries included African Americans, whites, and immigrants from other countries. In the woods and the sawmills the crews were often racially mixed, with the better-paying jobs ordinarily being held by whites, although there were exceptions. The sawyers and saw filers in the mills were considered skilled laborers, and were well paid by the standards of southern rural society during that era. Most jobs were for low wages, but any kind of job that offered a cash income was highly valued in a region and a time when rural folks, black and white, were accustomed to eking out only a meager existence. In fact, in some situations the workers were paid with company scrip or brozine, which was often honored at face value at the company store or commissary but discounted if used for purchases at other area establishments. The work in the woods and sawmills was physically tough and typically dangerous. Workers lost limbs and lives in a variety of ways—in the woods to felled trees or branches called "widow makers," to whirring saws and other machinery in the sawmills, on the logging trams, and on logging crews. Medical care was typically rudimentary, with the companies supplying physicians and deducting compulsory medical and accidental death and disability compensation premiums from the employees' wages. Workers in the naval stores industry were even more poorly paid and usually did not have the other benefits available to lumber company employees.

African American workers from the Lamb-Fish Lumber Company in Charleston, Mississippi, shooting craps, which a company advertising brochure termed "The African National Game." This Clifford H. Poland photograph shows the players using the "Hadden horn," a leather device used to tumble the dice and prevent cheating. It was invented by Memphis judge and mayor David Park Hadden.

Eastman-Gardiner Lumber Company shed crew in Laurel, Mississippi.

Workers at the R. F. Darrah Lumber Company in Meridian, Mississippi.

Workers at the
J. J. Newman Lumber
Company plant in Bude,
Mississippi, handling short-
leaf pine lumber.

Workers and camp cars at the Eastman-Gardiner
Lumber Company's Cohay Camp.

Eastman-Gardiner Lumber Company saw crew.

Logging crew and steam loader from Eastman-Gardiner
Lumber Company.

Saw filer in cutover woods.

Log cutters from the Foster Creek Lumber Company.

Sawyers with axes felling a tree in the Yazoo delta.

Clifford H. Poland was one of the first southern photographers to use a motion picture camera. Here Poland is shown taking a motion picture of Lamb-Fish Lumber Company sawyers using a crosscut saw to fell a tree.

Another Poland photograph of sawyers using a crosscut saw
and axes to fell a tree.

Loggers delimbing and "bucking" felled trees into log lengths.

Lamb-Fish Lumber Company workers using a cross-cut saw to cut an enormous hardwood tree into log lengths.

Workers crossloading logs onto truck.

Trainload of red gum from the Lamb-Fish Lumber Company destined for Europe.

Virtually from the beginning of commercial lumber production in Mississippi, part of the state's output was exported through Gulf Coast ports to markets in Europe and the Caribbean. Mississippi lumber was used in the construction of the Panama Canal, and during World War I Gulf Coast shipyards used Mississippi lumber to construct giant wooden ships for the Emergency Fleet Corporation. The exports included both pine and hardwoods. Mississippi's lumber producers again answered the call of war and turned out material for the construction of Camp Shelby and for other military uses during World War II.

Loading lumber for export at Gulfport, Mississippi.

Timber boom at Gulfport.

Unloading lumber at Gulfport.

Burns' Boom at Gulfport.

MOSS POINT, MISS. SCHOONER LOADING AT L. N. DANTZLER LUMBER CO'S MILL.   J. W. Stewart, Moss Point, Miss.

Schooner loading at L. N. Dantzler Lumber Company's
Moss Point mill.

10382. LOADING LUMBER ON STEAMER. GULFPORT. MISS.

Loading lumber at Gulfport.

Bierk & Blodgett Shipyard at Pascagoula, Mississippi.

Wooden ship construction scene.

Postcard scenes of Camp Shelby, Hattiesburg, Mississippi.

In the piney woods regions trees were tapped for turpentine production, an industry which was considered to have the worst working conditions among all of the forest products industries.

Pine trees tapped to collect gum for turpentine production.

Pine trees with "cups."

Turpentine woods crew.

"Dip squad" gathering gum for the Newton Naval Stores
Company near Wiggins, Mississippi, in 1948.

Worker from Newton Naval Stores Company scraping gum
from cup into bucket in 1950.

Turpentine distillery of the Finkbine Lumber Company, one
of the largest naval stores producers in Mississippi.

Turpentine still.

Interior view of Newton
Naval Stores Company still
in 1939.

Wood distillation plant at Columbia, Mississippi.
Photograph taken in April 1940.

Loading stumps at Bond, Mississippi, in 1939.

Turpentine was also produced by distilling it from stumps.

Weighing stumps for pine distillation in 1939.

Logs were also peeled and creosoted
for use as poles.

Peeling longleaf poles near
Brooklyn, Mississippi, in
1948.

Pole yard at Gulfport Creosoting Company north of
Wiggins in 1948.

Pine poles loaded on retort cars ready for creosote treatment at Crosby Lumber Company in 1939.

By the middle of the 1920s, vast areas of Mississippi's forests had been leveled by "cut out and get out" logging and lumber operations. The use of steam skidders and railroad logging left enormous expanses of largely treeless desolation. Wildfires ravaged the land, and, in areas bereft of grass and tree cover, erosion caused by Mississippi's torrential rains resulted in deep gullies and ravines. The creeks and rivers ran yellow and red and brown as the soil washed away and was floated downstream. People who flew across the South from the East Coast to the western extremities of the piney woods in east Texas remembered that they were never out of sight of fires. In some areas they could look for miles and see only idle land which had been totally stripped of trees.

Cutover land left by "skidder logging" in 1935.

Cutover lands.

Some of the lumber companies abandoned their land and let it revert to the state through nonpayment of taxes. Others established demonstration farms and tried to sell their denuded lands to farmers. Most of the land was best suited for growing trees, but there were efforts to raise cattle, grow various crops, and plant fruit and tung trees. These efforts generally met with only middling success at best. Some attempted to manufacture a variety of other products from the remaining timber supply.

Clearing Lamb-Fish Lumber Company cutover land for cultivation.

Cattle at Foster Creek Lumber Company Farm No. 2.

Peach Harvest Festival parade in Picayune,
Mississippi, in 1926.

First carload of strawberries shipped from Picayune,
Mississippi, in 1932.

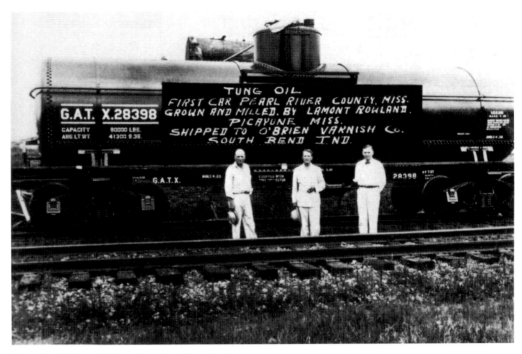

First carload of tung oil shipped from Pearl River County.

During the 1920s and 1930s small operators running portable "pecker-wood" or "groundhog" sawmills moved into the cutover areas and produced lumber from scattered patches of timber and even from areas that were considered denuded and commercially worthless by the large companies. These small mills have continued to produce significant quantities of lumber from that time to the present.

Oliver power plant at Perry Bowman mill near Caledonia, Mississippi.

Allis-Chalmers powered mill near Corinth, Mississippi.
Note the mules used for skidding at the mill site.

Logging truck belonging to W. C. Harmon of Aberdeen,
Mississippi.

Mill crew at the J. L. Lee sawmill near Carriere.

Eight-cylinder Nash automobile engine used as power plant
for Raymond Lumber Company mill at Raymond, Mississippi,
in 1937.

McCormick-Deering power plant at Lewis Brothers mill near
Gatesville, Mississippi, in 1937.

Mill crew at the Lewis Brothers mill near Gatesville,
Mississippi, in 1937.

Mill crew at S. C. Lowry Lumber Company near Moselle,
Mississippi.

Students at the Biltmore Forest School near Asheville, North Carolina, in 1910. The Biltmore school was funded by George Vanderbilt and led in its early period by famed German forester Carl Alwyn Schenck. He was followed by Gifford Pinchot.

The 1920s brought the development of the knowledge base and practical experience that would make reforestation and sustained-yield forest products operations possible in the South. Graduates from early forestry schools, particularly those at Biltmore and Yale, began to fan out across the South, and a few pioneering companies, such as the Crossett Lumber Company in Arkansas, Henry Hardtner's Urania Lumber Company in Louisiana, the Great Southern Lumber Company with lands in both Mississippi and Louisiana, and the Crosby Lumber Company and H. Weston Lumber Company in Mississippi, struggled to keep going and to provide for the reforestation of their lands. The Yale Forestry School ran summer forestry camps for its students at Urania and at Crossett, Arkansas, and the idea took hold that the South was the place to be for young foresters who wanted to do something productive and significant with their lives and careers.

Henry E. Hardtner of Louisiana's Urania Lumber Company hosted the summer camps of the Yale Forestry School and provided an early example of practical reforestation that inspired emulators across the South.

Frank Ostin ("Red") Bateman was a self-trained pioneer forester who directed the massive Great Southern Lumber Company tree planting program in Louisiana and Mississippi during the early 1920s.

J. Roland Weston claimed to be the first professionally trained forester in Mississippi. Graduating from the University of Washington in 1921, Weston believed he was the first native Mississippian to earn a forestry degree, and said that when he came home to work for the family there was only one other forestry graduate in the state.

Self-trained pioneer forester Posey Howell became a legend in the Mississippi forestry community. He is shown here in 1948 presenting diplomas to graduates of an Illinois Central Railroad forestry short course. Howell is second from the left, and Illinois Central Railroad forester John Guthrie is third from the left.

The first dean of Mississippi State University's School of Forest Resources was Dr. Robert T. Clapp. In this 1969 photograph, Clapp, in the center, is flanked on the left by Mississippi Commissioner of Agriculture Jim Buck Ross, and on the right by Dr. Rodney Foil, who later headed the forestry school.

Forestry education at Mississippi A&M (now Mississippi State University) began with the employment of the first forester in 1905. The school began granting forestry degrees in 1954.

The School of Forest Resources building at Mississippi State University was constructed in the 1990s.

Polly Anderson was the first woman graduate of the Mississippi State University School of Forest Resources. She is pictured above in a 1973 photograph from the Mississippi State University yearbook, and on the right in a recent photograph with her daughters.

Portrait of Mrs. G. L. (Maud Celeste Colmer) Reeves.

An important step toward the recovery of Mississippi's forests was the establishment of the Mississippi Forestry Commission in 1926. Escatawpa native Mrs. G. L. (Maud Celeste Colmer) Reeves of Jackson was instrumental in the establishment of the agency. She was one of its original members, and later was education director and editor of the commission's monthly publication. She was also related by marriage to pioneer forester Posey Howell. Roy L. Hogue, trained at the University of Michigan, was the first Mississippi State Forester.

Roy L. Hogue served as the first Mississippi State Forester.

The members of the Mississippi Forestry Commission inspecting work at Bogalusa, Louisiana. Photograph taken on June 13, 1928.

Most foresters agreed that, beyond the lack of silvicultural knowledge, the two greatest obstacles in the way of southern reforestation were razorback hogs and fire. Posey Howell followed a razorback hog and found that the hog could root up more pine seedlings in a day than Howell's crews could plant in a week. Natural fires and conflagrations set by arsonists devastated southern forests. The South had the highest arson rate in the country, and in the 1940s L. O. Crosby, Jr., remembered that arsonists destroyed so much timber that for a time he gave up on reforestation.

Razorback hogs. The scourge of the southern pineries.

Fighting fire with pine tops.

Technological innovation was important in the efforts at fire control. At first people fought fires by trying to beat them out with pine tops, or "fire flaps." Over time, modern equipment including fire-spotting towers, airplanes for aerial surveillance and the spraying of chemical fire retardants, two-way radios, fire plows, portable backpack pumps, and mobile equipment came into use.

Man using pine top to fight fire.

Early firefighter with equipment.

Early primitive fire tower.

Lane Fire Tower in Jefferson Davis County was fifty feet in height.

Woodall Fire Tower, the highest point in Mississippi at 806 feet.

Fire tower personnel in the DeSoto National Forest in 1948.

Art Nelson of the Flintkote Company was a pioneer in the use of two-way radio. Nelson is shown here with an early experimental set.

L. O. Crosby, Jr., of the Crosby Forest Products Company of Picayune, with Mrs. Lucile S. Hopkins, who dispatched messages to the forestry crews from the central station.

Early Mississippi Forestry Commission airplane.

The L. N. Dantzler Lumber Company used one of the first
airplanes to spot fires in south Mississippi. Shown here at
Wiggins in Stone County, in 1951, is pilot Sonny Holliman,
with Ollie Reeves in the Jeep.

A Mississippi Forestry Commission contracted helicopter used for spraying herbicides, aerial seeding, spotting fires, and directing firefighting crews.

Firefighters with portable backpack pumps.

Mississippi Forestry Commission Jeep with fire plow.

In addition to the detection and fighting of fires, education was a key to prevention and control. The American Forestry Association sent trucks across the South with rangers called the Dixie Crusaders, who showed movies and slides preaching fire prevention to schoolchildren and the members of community organizations. The United States Forest Service ran a similar program.

American Forestry Association truck at Bay Springs, Mississippi.

United States Forest Service truck used in educational programs.

CREW OF 250 FARMER MEN & BOYS
PLANTING 180000 PINE TREES DAILY
G.S.L.G DEC 12-1925 BOGALUSA La

Great Southern Lumber Company planting crews in 1925.

The third part of the trilogy that was basic to the reforestation of Mississippi and the rest of the South was planting. Without hog control and fire prevention, planting was futile. When the practice of leaving seed trees after logging was carried out, some forests reseeded naturally. Others were seeded, sometimes by aircraft. Many were reforested by the planting of seedlings by hand with a spade-like tool called a dibble. Later planting was revolutionized by the development of planting machines that were pulled by tractors or Jeeps.

The mechanical planter that was widely used across the South evolved from a machine developed by Professor Daniel DenUyl of the Purdue University School of Forestry. When John Guthrie, a Purdue forestry student, graduated, he went to work as a forester for the Illinois Central Railroad. The Illinois Central, like some other railroads, promoted forestry work in the South in order to generate traffic. Guthrie remembered the Purdue planting machine and arranged for its shipment to Mississippi, where it was modified in the Illinois Central shops at McComb. The machine became known as the Illinois Central Tree Planter. Guthrie, because of his promotion of forestry and planting, was dubbed "Johnny Pinetree" by the newspapers of nearby New Orleans.

The Purdue planter just after arrival at the Illinois Central Railroad station in Hattiesburg, Mississippi, in November 1948. John Guthrie is on the right with a group of Hattiesburg businessmen.

John Guthrie seated on the modified machine, now known as the Illinois Central Tree Planter, in early 1949.

The federal government, the Mississippi Forestry Commission, and private companies established nurseries to supply seedlings for the planting effort.

Nursery workers sorting seedlings.

Worker grading and counting seedlings at the Mississippi Forestry Commission nursery at Mt. Olive.

Harvesting seedlings at a state nursery.

Mississippi Forestry Commission shipment of
"baby trees."

One of the major contributors to the recovery of the Mississippi forest products industry was William T. Mason of Laurel, who invented the pressed-wood product sold under the brand name Masonite.

Portrait of William T. Mason.

Blowtorch and press used by William T. Mason in the process of inventing Masonite.

Mason Fiber Company plant at Laurel, Mississippi.

Masonite Corporation plant at Laurel in 1948.

Charles Holmes Herty perfected the chemical process which made it possible to utilize southern pine pulp to manufacture newsprint.

During the 1930s the growing abundance of young trees on Mississippi's cutover lands, plus the technological contributions of scientists like Charles Holmes Herty, paved the way for the rise of the pulp and paper industry. The industry became a staple of Mississippi's economy. Utilizing young growth, the industry created a new market for timberland owners and employment opportunities for professional foresters, while contributing to the success of forest management. However, in the early years foresters from the lumber companies looked upon those working for the pulp and paper industry with suspicion.

Early pulpwood thinning, with the logs stacked in "pens," a pen being the standard unit of measure for pulpwood. While these logs were cut by a saw, the work was often done with an axe. These pens are in the Homochitto National Forest in 1939.

Pulpwood truck and crew in the woods.

The Southern Kraft Paper Corporation plant at Moss Point in 1939.

Early postcard view of the machine room at the Southern Kraft Paper Corporation mill at Moss Point.

MACHINE ROOM, SOUTHERN PAPER CO., MOSS POINT, MISS.

Pulpwood trucks at wood yard in 1950s. The truck in the foreground appears to be from Natalbany, Louisiana, near the Mississippi state line.

In 1933 the federal government established one of President Franklin Delano Roosevelt's best-known New Deal agencies, the Tennessee Valley Authority, with a mission of flood control and navigation improvement, power generation, and regional economic development in the Tennessee River valley. As part of its effort to restore the region's lands, TVA established nurseries to provide seedlings for area reforestation. Later the agency transferred some of its lands to Mississippi for the establishment of state parks.

Paper-making machine at Weyerhaeuser's Columbus, Mississippi, complex. This machine could produce a twenty-four-foot ribbon of paper, nine hundred miles long, every twenty-four hours.

Mississippi Forestry Commission truck loading seedlings at the TVA nursery at Wilson Dam, Alabama, for distribution in Tishomingo County, Mississippi.

J. P. Coleman State Park on Pickwick Lake near Iuka in
Tishomingo County. The park was created from TVA lands.

During the 1930s the United States Forest Service established the Southern Hardwoods Laboratory at Stoneville to experiment with the cultivation and use of hardwoods. John A. Putnam, the first leader of the laboratory, became known across Mississippi and the South as "Mr. Hardwoods." His successor, J. S. McKnight, also became a prominent leader in the hardwood community. The Mississippi Forestry Commission also encouraged the planting of hardwoods in appropriate areas.

Portrait of John A. Putnam.

Portrait of J. S. McKnight.

The Southern Hardwoods Laboratory at Stoneville, Mississippi.

Harvesting cottonwood cuttings at the Mississippi Forestry Commission's Winona nursery. Cottonwoods can be used as pulpwood for the production of magazine-quality paper.

The Mississippi Forestry Association, founded in 1937, has been a major force since that time in promoting reforestation, fire control, responsible forest management, and forestry education and training. It has represented the forestry community through public relations work and governmental lobbying.

During the 1930s the federal government established national forests in Mississippi, mainly on cutover lands. Nurseries were set up that contributed to Mississippi's reforestation, provided recreational opportunities, and furnished timber for the forest products industry.

Frank B. Pittman, a native of Wayne County, Mississippi, and a graduate of Mississippi A&M (now Mississippi State University), was the Mississippi Forestry Association's first executive secretary.

Ray Conarro was the first supervisor of the Mississippi national forests.

Cutover lands in DeSoto National Forest in 1937.

Longleaf pine seedbeds in the DeSoto National Forest in 1937.

CCC corpsmen in the DeSoto National Forest.

CCC corpsmen and camp commanders at Camp F-4 at
Richton, Mississippi, in 1934.

CCC pile-driving crew.

CCC radio repair class.

The Civilian Conservation Corps was another New Deal agency that did important work in the restoration of Mississippi's forests during the 1930s. Created in 1933, the CCC took unemployed young men from the cities and put them to work at various jobs in the nation's forests and parks under a military type of structure. There were ninety-five camps in Mississippi—twenty-six categorized as forest camps, ten as state park camps, nine as military park camps, twenty-three as private land camps, and twenty-seven as conservation camps.

CCC planting crew.

CCC corpsmen moving a log.

CCC barracks at camp in Tishomingo County.

Saturday barracks inspection at Camp F-4.

CCC Co. 442 baseball team.

The federal government implemented flood control and reforestation programs in the watershed of the Yazoo and Little Tallahatchie rivers in 1944. Many of the lands in the area of the Yazoo–Little Tallahatchie (YLT) Flood Control Project were both deforested and badly eroded. The Soil Conservation Service supervised the project, and during the period from 1948 to 1985 the U.S. Forest Service carried out what has been described as the largest tree planting program in the nation's history.

Construction of Sardis Dam was part of the YLT project.

Eroded YLT area lands.

Female planting crew with dibbles in Calhoun County, Mississippi.

Planting crew with dibbles on YLT project.

Before and after.
An eroded hillside
near Taylor, Mississippi,
in 1948.

The same hillside in 1957,
nine years after being
planted with loblolly pine.

Farmer W. C. Turpin of
Lafayette County in the YLT
area, shown with dibble and
seedlings. Turpin plants on
the hillside, while his
brother Fred plows with
mules in the valley.

The United States mobilization effort during World War II involved using Mississippi's recovering forests to furnish wood for the construction of military bases and to supply the armed forces with various products. Preventing and fighting woods fires now became a patriotic obligation.

U.S. Forest Service fire prevention poster.

Southern pine was used to construct barracks at Dodd Field in San Antonio and at other bases.

Boxes made of southern pine were used to package equipment for the U.S. Army Signal Corps.

Warren A. Hood. Photograph taken in the early 1940s.

Jim Craig was Mississippi State Forester from 1952 until 1955. He was born in Panola County.

During the postwar period native Mississippian Warren A. Hood built a forest products empire.

James W. Craig, a native Mississippian and graduate of Purdue University and the New York State College of Forestry, became Mississippi State Forester and founded one of the forestry profession's major supply houses.

In the 1940s the tree farm movement came to Mississippi, and it has been an important force in restoring and maintaining the state's forests since that time. Mississippi has long been the nation's leading tree farm state.

Pioneer forester Richard C. Allen of the A. DeWeese Lumber Company in Philadelphia, Mississippi, is pictured on the company's forty-thousand-acre tree farm. A native Mississippian trained at the University of Georgia, Dick Allen went on to a long career with Weyerhaeuser and later served with distinction as Mississippi State Forester.

Tree farm. Note that in this photograph the trees are of a single species (pine) and a uniform age. They are planted in rows as a tree plantation. Some environmentalists charge that such forests are inferior on both biological and aesthetic grounds to natural mixed-aged and mixed-species forests.

Selective cutting on Denkmann Lumber Company lands in Leake County, Mississippi, with one-third of the stand removed.

Unthinned stand of loblolly pine in the Bienville District of the DeSoto National Forest in 1948.

A standard technique of good forest management is thinning the forest through periodic selective cutting.

Thinned loblolly stand in the Bienville District of the DeSoto National Forest in 1948. Slightly over seven cords per acre were cut; twelve cords per acre remain.

As part of its campaign to promote forestry, the Mississippi Forestry Commission sponsored a Queen of the Forest competition during the 1950s and 1960s. Undoubtedly the most famous Queen of the Forest was Brandon's Mary Ann Mobley, the 1954 winner, who went on to become Miss America and then embarked on an acting career in Hollywood.

Mary Ann Mobley as Queen of the Forest in 1954.

Plywood joined the family of Mississippi forest products during the 1950s, while the naval stores industry promoted getting money from "the trees of the past" and improving the land through removing stumps. Production of wood veneers also became an important industry.

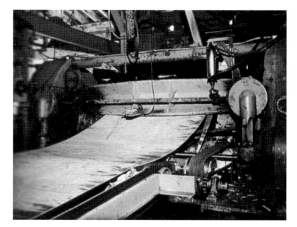

Plywood machine.

The Hercules Powder Company promotes stump removal.

Veneer logs at the Mengel Company in Laurel are being loaded into steam vat tanks which steam them in preparation for being cut into veneer sheets.

Giant trucks haul logs from the woods to the mill.

Hurricane Camille damage.

Possibly the greatest natural disaster to hit Mississippi's forests in modern times was Hurricane Camille, which devastated the southern part of the state in 1969. Described as the worst hurricane ever to hit North America, Camille pounded the Gulf Coast with winds in excess of two hundred miles per hour and damaged vast quantities of timber.

Downed and splintered trees damaged by Hurricane Camille.

The forest products industry has made great technological progress in the woods and in plants and mills. From the development of genetically altered seedlings which grow faster and straighter to the use of computers and scanners which analyze logs entering the mill and regulate the processing machinery, technology has significantly altered life and work in Mississippi's forests and mills.

International Paper Company's pioneering Buschcombine was a multipurpose machine that felled the tree, debarked it, cut it into pulping-length logs, or "sticks," and then bucked and bunched its load.

Unloading logs at the mill.

Logs entering a mill are scanned and analyzed for optimum use. These are the controls in a modern computerized mill.

Since 1987 the Mississippi Forestry Commission, the Mississippi Forestry Association, and the national forests in Mississippi have sponsored Mississippi's participation in a national environmental education program called Project Learning Tree (PLT). The program trains teachers, natural resource professionals, and youth group leaders who bring environmental education to students from grades pre-K to twelve. By 1998 over 250 volunteer facilitators of the program had been trained in Mississippi. Longtime Mississippi Forestry Commission employee Bill Colvin coordinated the PLT program from its inception and became known as "Mr. PLT."

Bill Colvin (left) and Mississippi State Forester Jim Sledge at the time of Colvin's retirement in 1998.

Certification in the Sustainable Forestry Initiative became a marketing tool for loggers.

As part of the effort to improve the forest products industry's image and practices, the Mississippi Forestry Association sponsored and Mississippi State University conducted training programs through which loggers could become certified in the Sustainable Forestry Initiative, denoting that they operated responsibly.

The T. M. S. chip mill in Louisville, Mississippi, in about 1995.

Environmentalists have continued to be critical of the replacement of mixed-species and mixed-aged forests by even-aged pine plantations. They also charge that the forest products industry is not sufficiently concerned about such matters as the protection of endangered species like the red-cockaded woodpecker, the use of chemical herbicides, and the proliferation of gigantic chip mills which consume prodigious quantities of wood. They continue to complain about the ugliness of clearcuts and the impact on water quality on lands which are left bereft of cover. National forests, they say, have been little more than timber factories for the forest products industry. The forest products industry has recognized the growing public insistence on having a voice in determining how the nation's forests, public and private, will be managed. Foresters and the forest products industry have responded to these concerns with a number of public relations programs and initiatives. Also, money that was made from forest products has been used in various philanthropic ways, including the establishment of wilderness preserves and recreational and environmental facilities.

Red-cockaded woodpecker.

Pondberry is among the endangered plant species that are being studied in Mississippi's forests.

The Louisiana black bear restoration program is well under way in Mississippi.

Champion International Corporation endangered species brochure.

Monsanto herbicide brochure.

Pinecote, the native plant center of the Crosby Arboretum at Picayune, one of the most visible of the Crosby family's many philanthropies in Mississippi.

Today, retailers like Wal-Mart and Home Depot attempt, with mixed success, to address the growing public concern over environmental issues. They advertise that they sell forest products that are certified as having been responsibly harvested and manufactured. This process is called "green certification."

"Sustainable Forestry" is today's industry slogan for responsible forest practice.

Georgia-Pacific brochure.

Home Depot advertisement.

Credits

p. 2 — Courtesy of East Texas Research Center, Ralph W. Steen Library, Stephen F. Austin State University.

p. 3 — Courtesy of East Texas Research Center, Ralph W. Steen Library, Stephen F. Austin State University.

p. 4, top — Courtesy of Mississippi Forestry Commission.

p. 4, bottom — Photograph by Sidney Streater for *American Lumberman*. Courtesy of Forest History Society.

p. 5, top — From George Harvey's *Harvey's Scenes in the Primeval Forests of America* (London, 1841). Courtesy of the American Philosophical Society.

p. 5, bottom — Illustration from *Das Illustrite Mississippithal*, Henry Lewis, American, 1819–1904. St. Louis Art Museum photograph.

p. 6, top — Drawing by Bruce Lyndon Cunningham in Robert S. Maxwell and Robert D. Baker, *Sawdust Empire* (College Station: Texas A&M University Press, 1983). Use of the drawing is by courtesy of the artist.

p. 6, bottom — Courtesy of Forest History Society.

p. 7, top — Courtesy of Dr. Brian Roy Lockhart.

p. 7, center — Portrait of Andrew Brown in John Hebron Moore, *Andrew Brown and Cypress Lumbering in the Old Southwest* (Baton Rouge: Louisiana State University Press, 1967).

p. 7, bottom — Photograph of Henry Weston. Courtesy of the Weston family.

p. 8, top — Photograph in Gilbert H. Hoffman, *Dummy Lines through the Longleaf: A History of the Sawmills and Logging Railroads of Southwest Mississippi* (Oxford: Center for the Study of Southern Culture, University of Mississippi, 1992), 7.

p. 8, bottom — Courtesy of Lauren Rogers Museum of Art Library, Laurel, Mississippi.

p. 9, top — Photograph reproduced from *Economic Botany of Alabama, Part I, Monograph 8, Geological Survey of Alabama* (1913) in Nollie Hickman, *Mississippi Harvest* (University, Mississippi: University of Mississippi, 1962).

p. 9, bottom — Photograph by John N. Teunisson, New Orleans, Louisiana. Courtesy of McCain Library and Archives, University of Southern Mississippi.

p. 10, top — Courtesy of Lauren Rogers Museum of Art Library, Laurel, Mississippi.

p. 10, bottom — Courtesy of Lauren Rogers Museum of Art Library, Laurel, Mississippi.

p. 11, top — Courtesy of Lauren Rogers Museum of Art Library, Laurel, Mississippi.

p. 11, bottom — Courtesy of Lauren Rogers Museum of Art Library, Laurel, Mississippi.

p. 12, top — Courtesy of Lauren Rogers Museum of Art Library, Laurel, Mississippi.

p. 12, bottom — Courtesy of Lauren Rogers Museum of Art Library, Laurel, Mississippi.

p. 13, top — Courtesy of Mississippi Department of Archives and History, Jackson, Mississippi.

p. 13, bottom — Courtesy of Lauren Rogers Museum of Art Library, Laurel, Mississippi.

p. 14, top — Courtesy of Arthur M. Nelson, Jr.

p. 14, bottom — Courtesy of Forest History Society.

p. 15, top — Photograph from a lantern slide in Forest History Society Collection.

p. 15, bottom — Courtesy of Lauren Rogers Museum of Art Library, Laurel, Mississippi.

p. 16 — Courtesy of Lauren Rogers Museum of Art Library, Laurel, Mississippi.

p. 17, top — Courtesy of Lauren Rogers Museum of Art Library, Laurel, Mississippi.

p. 17, bottom — Courtesy of Mississippi Forestry Commission.

p. 18, top — Photograph by Clifford H. Poland. Courtesy of the Memphis Room, Memphis Public Library.

p. 18, bottom — Courtesy of Mississippi Department of Archives and History, Jackson, Mississippi.

p. 19, top — Photograph by Clifford H. Poland. Courtesy of the Memphis Room, Memphis Public Library.

p. 19, center — Photograph by Clifford H. Poland. Courtesy of the Memphis Room, Memphis Public Library.

p. 19, bottom left — Photograph by Clifford H. Poland. Courtesy of the Memphis Room, Memphis Public Library.

p. 19, bottom right — Courtesy of Forest History Society.

p. 20 — Courtesy of Mississippi Forestry Commission.

p. 21, top	U.S. Forest Service photograph. Courtesy of Mississippi Forestry Commission.	p. 32, top	Courtesy of Mississippi Forestry Commission.
p. 21, bottom	Courtesy of Mississippi Forestry Commission.	p. 32, bottom	Courtesy of Mississippi Forestry Commission.
p. 22, top	Photograph by Clifford H. Poland. Courtesy of the Memphis Room, Memphis Public Library.	p. 33, top	Courtesy of Anderson-Tully Lumber Company.
p. 22, bottom	Courtesy of Lauren Rogers Museum of Art Library, Laurel, Mississippi.	p. 33, bottom	Photograph by W. H. Marin. Courtesy of U.S. Forest Service, Jackson, Mississippi.
p. 23, top	Courtesy of Lauren Rogers Museum of Art Library, Laurel, Mississippi.	p. 34, top	Courtesy of Anderson-Tully Lumber Company.
p. 23, bottom	Photograph by Clifford H. Poland. Courtesy of the Memphis Room, Memphis Public Library.	p. 34 and 35, center	Courtesy of the Weston family.
		p. 35, top	Photograph in John Hebron Moore, *Andrew Brown and Cypress Lumbering in the Old Southwest* (Baton Rouge: Louisiana State University Press, 1967).
p. 24, top	Photograph by Clifford H. Poland. Courtesy of the Memphis Room, Memphis Public Library.		
p. 24, bottom	Courtesy of Mississippi Department of Archives and History, Jackson, Mississippi.	p. 35, bottom	Courtesy of Forest History Society.
		p. 36, top	Courtesy of Forest History Society.
p. 25	Courtesy of Lauren Rogers Museum of Art Library, Laurel, Mississippi.	p. 36, bottom	Courtesy of Lauren Rogers Museum of Art Library, Laurel, Mississippi.
p. 26, top	Photograph by Clifford H. Poland. Courtesy of the Memphis Room, Memphis Public Library.	p. 37, top	Photograph by Clifford H. Poland. Courtesy of the Memphis Room, Memphis Public Library.
p. 26, bottom	Courtesy of Mississippi Forestry Commission.	p. 37, bottom	Photograph by Clifford H. Poland. Courtesy of the Memphis Room, Memphis Public Library.
p. 27, top	Courtesy of Lauren Rogers Museum of Art Library, Laurel, Mississippi.	p. 38, top left	Courtesy of Anderson-Tully Lumber Company.
p. 27, bottom	Courtesy of Mississippi Forestry Commission.	p. 38, top right	Courtesy of Anderson-Tully Lumber Company.
p. 28, top	Courtesy of Lauren Rogers Museum of Art Library, Laurel, Mississippi.	p. 38, bottom	Photograph in *American Lumberman*, no. 2561 (June 14, 1924), 57.
p. 28, bottom	Courtesy of Special Collections Department, Mitchell Memorial Library, Mississippi State University.	p. 39	Photograph by Clifford H. Poland. Courtesy of the Memphis Room, Memphis Public Library.
p. 29, top	Photograph by Clifford H. Poland. Courtesy of the Memphis Room, Memphis Public Library.	p. 40, top	Photograph by Clifford H. Poland. Courtesy of the Memphis Room, Memphis Public Library.
p. 29, bottom	Photograph by John N. Teunisson, New Orleans, Louisiana. Courtesy of McCain Library and Archives, University of Southern Mississippi.	p. 40, bottom	Photograph by Clifford H. Poland. Courtesy of the Memphis Room, Memphis Public Library.
		p. 41, top left	Courtesy of the Department of Archives and Manuscripts, Louisiana State University.
p. 30, top	Courtesy of McCain Library and Archives, University of Southern Mississippi.	p. 41, top center	Courtesy of the Center for the Study of Southern Culture, University of Mississippi. This portrait hangs in the Mississippi Hall of Fame in the Old Capitol Museum, Jackson.
p. 30, bottom	Photograph by Clifford H. Poland. Courtesy of the Memphis Room, Memphis Public Library.		
p. 31, top	Courtesy of Lauren Rogers Museum of Art Library, Laurel, Mississippi.	p. 41, top right	Photograph in *Southern Lumberman*, Vol. 144, No. 1817 (December 15, 1931), 113.
p. 31, bottom	Photograph by Bluford W. Muir. Courtesy of U.S. Forest Service, Jackson, Mississippi.	p. 41, bottom	Courtesy of Donald S. Bell.
		p. 42, left	Courtesy of Donald S. Bell.
		p. 42, center	Courtesy of Anderson-Tully Lumber Company.

p. 42, right	Photograph in Jim Fisher, *Gilchrist: The First Fifty Years* (Bend, OR: Oregon Color Press, 1988).	p. 55, top	Photograph in *From Tree to Trade* (Kansas City: The Long-Bell Lumber Company, 1920), 6.
p. 43	Photograph in John Hebron Moore, *Andrew Brown and Cypress Lumbering in the Old Southwest* (Baton Rouge: Louisiana State University Press, 1967).	p. 55, bottom	Courtesy of Mississippi Department of Archives and History, Jackson, Mississippi.
p. 44, top	Photograph in *American Lumberman*, no. 2561 (June 14, 1924), 56.	p. 56, top	Photograph by Clifford H. Poland in *Lamb-Fish Lumber Company: The Hardwood Lumber and Farming Industries of Mississippi* (Panama Pacific Exposition, San Francisco, California, 1915), 50.
p. 44, bottom	Cooper Postcard Collection. Courtesy of Mississippi Department of Archives and History, Jackson, Mississippi.	p. 56, bottom	Photograph by Clifford H. Poland in *Lamb-Fish Lumber Company: The Hardwood Lumber and Farming Industries of Mississippi* (Panama Pacific Exposition, San Francisco, California, 1915), 48.
p. 45, top	Courtesy of McCain Library and Archives, University of Southern Mississippi.		
p. 45, bottom	Photograph by W. H. Marin, U.S. Forest Service. Courtesy of Forest History Society.	p. 57, top	Courtesy of Lauren Rogers Museum of Art Library, Laurel, Mississippi.
p. 46	Photograph by Donald S. Bell. Courtesy of Donald S. Bell.	p. 57, bottom	Photograph in *American Lumberman*, no. 2561 (June 14, 1924), 53.
p. 47	Courtesy of Lauren Rogers Museum of Art Library, Laurel, Mississippi.	p. 58, top	Courtesy of Mississippi Department of Archives and History, Jackson, Mississippi.
p. 48 and 49, top	Courtesy of the Weston family.	p. 58, center	Courtesy of Mississippi Department of Archives and History, Jackson, Mississippi.
p. 49, bottom	Courtesy of Lauren Rogers Museum of Art Library, Laurel, Mississippi.	p. 58, bottom	Courtesy of Mississippi Department of Archives and History, Jackson, Mississippi.
p. 50, top	Cooper Postcard Collection. Courtesy of Mississippi Department of Archives and History, Jackson, Mississippi.	p. 59	Courtesy of Lauren Rogers Museum of Art Library, Laurel, Mississippi.
p. 50, bottom	Photograph in *From Tree to Trade* (Kansas City: The Long-Bell Lumber Company, 1920), 15.	p. 60, top	Courtesy of Lauren Rogers Museum of Art Library, Laurel, Mississippi.
p. 51	Photograph by John N. Teunisson, New Orleans, Louisiana. Courtesy of McCain Library and Archives, University of Southern Mississippi.	p. 60, center	Courtesy of Mississippi Department of Archives and History, Jackson, Mississippi.
p. 52, top	Photograph by John N. Teunisson, New Orleans, Louisiana. Courtesy of McCain Library and Archives, University of Southern Mississippi.	p. 60, bottom	Courtesy of Mississippi Department of Archives and History, Jackson, Mississippi.
p. 52, bottom	Photograph by John N. Teunisson, New Orleans, Louisiana. Courtesy of McCain Library and Archives, University of Southern Mississippi.	p. 61	Photograph in *American Lumberman*, no. 2561 (June 14, 1924), 59.
p. 53, top	Courtesy of Anderson-Tully Lumber Company.	p. 62, top	Courtesy of Lauren Rogers Museum of Art Library, Laurel, Mississippi.
p. 53, center	Cooper Postcard Collection. Courtesy of Mississippi Department of Archives and History, Jackson, Mississippi.	p. 62, bottom	Courtesy of Mississippi Forestry Commission.
p. 53, bottom	Cooper Postcard Collection. Courtesy of Mississippi Department of Archives and History, Jackson, Mississippi.	p. 63, top	Courtesy of Lauren Rogers Museum of Art Library, Laurel, Mississippi.
		p. 63, bottom	Photograph by Clifford H. Poland. Courtesy of the Memphis Room, Memphis Public Library.
p. 54, top	Photograph in *American Lumberman*, no. 2561 (June 14, 1924), 60.	p. 64	Courtesy of Lauren Rogers Museum of Art Library, Laurel, Mississippi.
p. 54, bottom	Courtesy of Mississippi Department of Archives and History, Jackson, Mississippi.	p. 65, top	Courtesy of Forest History Society.

p. 65, center	Courtesy of the Center for the Study of Southern Culture, University of Mississippi.	p. 77, top	Courtesy of East Texas Research Center, Ralph W. Steen Library, Stephen F. Austin State University.
p. 65, bottom	Photograph by John N. Teunisson, New Orleans, Louisiana. Courtesy of McCain Library and Archives, University of Southern Mississippi.	p. 77, center	Photograph by Clifford H. Poland. Courtesy of the Memphis Room, Memphis Public Library.
p. 66, top	Courtesy of Forest History Society.	p. 77, bottom	In Thomas D. Clark, *The Greening of the South: The Recovery of Land and Forest* (Lexington: University Press of Kentucky, 1984). Courtesy of Kentucky Division of Forestry.
p. 66, bottom	Courtesy of Mississippi Department of Archives and History, Jackson, Mississippi.		
p. 67, top	Courtesy of Lauren Rogers Museum of Art Library, Laurel, Mississippi.	p. 78, top	Photograph by Clifford H. Poland. Courtesy of the Memphis Room, Memphis Public Library.
p. 67, bottom	Courtesy of Mississippi Department of Archives and History, Jackson, Mississippi.	p. 78, bottom	Cooper Postcard Collection. Courtesy of Mississippi Department of Archives and History, Jackson, Mississippi.
p. 68, top	Courtesy of Lauren Rogers Museum of Art Library, Laurel, Mississippi.	p. 79, top	Cooper Postcard Collection. Courtesy of Mississippi Department of Archives and History, Jackson, Mississippi.
p. 68, bottom	Courtesy of Mississippi Department of Archives and History, Jackson, Mississippi.	p. 79, center	Cooper Postcard Collection. Courtesy of Mississippi Department of Archives and History, Jackson, Mississippi.
p. 69, top	Courtesy of Lauren Rogers Museum of Art Library, Laurel, Mississippi.		
p. 69, bottom	Courtesy of Lauren Rogers Museum of Art Library, Laurel, Mississippi.	p. 79, bottom	Cooper Postcard Collection. Courtesy of Mississippi Department of Archives and History, Jackson, Mississippi.
p. 70, top	Photograph by Clifford H. Poland. Courtesy of the Memphis Room, Memphis Public Library.	p. 80	Cooper Postcard Collection. Courtesy of Mississippi Department of Archives and History, Jackson, Mississippi.
p. 70, bottom	Courtesy of Lauren Rogers Museum of Art Library, Laurel, Mississippi.	p. 81	Cooper Postcard Collection. Courtesy of Mississippi Department of Archives and History, Jackson, Mississippi.
p. 71, top	Courtesy of Forest History Society.		
p. 71, bottom	Courtesy of Forest History Society.	p. 82, top	Courtesy of McCain Library and Archives, University of Southern Mississippi.
p. 72	Courtesy of Lauren Rogers Museum of Art Library, Laurel, Mississippi.	p. 82, bottom	Courtesy of Department of Archives and Manuscripts, Louisiana State University.
p. 73, top	Courtesy of Lauren Rogers Museum of Art Library, Laurel, Mississippi.	p. 83, top	Courtesy of McCain Library and Archives, University of Southern Mississippi.
p. 73, bottom	Courtesy of Lauren Rogers Museum of Art Library, Laurel, Mississippi.	p. 83, center	U.S. Forest Service Photograph. Courtesy of Mississippi Forestry Commission.
p. 74, top	Courtesy of Mississippi Forestry Commission.	p. 83, bottom	U.S. Forest Service photograph. Courtesy of Mississippi Forestry Commission.
p. 74, bottom	Courtesy of Mississippi Department of Archives and History, Jackson, Mississippi.		
p. 75, top	Photograph by Clifford H. Poland. Courtesy of the Memphis Room, Memphis Public Library.	p. 84, top	Photograph courtesy of Library of Congress.
p. 75, bottom	Photograph by Clifford H. Poland. Courtesy of the Memphis Room, Memphis Public Library.	p. 84, bottom	Photograph by Bluford W. Muir. Courtesy of U.S. Forest Service, Jackson, Mississippi.
p. 76	Photograph by Clifford H. Poland. Courtesy of the Memphis Room, Memphis Public Library.	p. 85	Photograph by Bluford W. Muir. Courtesy of U.S. Forest Service, Jackson, Mississippi.

p. 86, top	Collection of Mrs. J. A. Simpson. In Nollie Hickman, *Mississippi Harvest* (University, Mississippi: University of Mississippi, 1962).
p. 86, bottom	Courtesy of the Crosby Arboretum, Picayune, Mississippi.
p. 87, top	Photograph by W. H. Marin. Courtesy of U.S. Forest Service, Jackson, Mississippi.
p. 87, bottom	Courtesy of Mississippi Forestry Commission.
p. 88, top	Photograph by W. H. Marin. Courtesy of U.S. Forest Service, Jackson, Mississippi.
p. 88, bottom	Photograph by W. H. Marin. Courtesy of U.S. Forest Service, Jackson, Mississippi.
p. 89, top	Photograph by Bluford W. Muir. Courtesy of U.S. Forest Service, Jackson, Mississippi.
p. 89, bottom	Photograph by Bluford W. Muir. Courtesy of U.S. Forest Service, Jackson, Mississippi.
p. 90	Photograph by W. H. Marin. Courtesy of U.S. Forest Service, Jackson, Mississippi.
p. 91, top	Photograph by Carter. Courtesy of U.S. Forest Service, Jackson, Mississippi.
p. 91, bottom	Photograph in *The South's Fourth Forest: Opportunities to Increase the Resource Wealth of the South*, United States Department of Agriculture, Forest Service, Forest Resource Miscellaneous Publication No. 1461 (Washington, 1988), 14.
p. 92, top	Photograph by Clifford H. Poland. Courtesy of the Memphis Room, Memphis Public Library.
p. 92, bottom	Courtesy of Mississippi Department of Archives and History, Jackson, Mississippi.
p. 93, top	Courtesy of the Historic Photograph Collection, Margaret Reed Crosby Memorial Library, Picayune, Mississippi.
p. 93, bottom	Courtesy of the Center for the Study of Southern Culture, University of Mississippi.
p. 94, top	Courtesy of the Historic Photograph Collection, Margaret Reed Crosby Memorial Library, Picayune, Mississippi.
p. 94, bottom	Courtesy of James E. Fickle.
p. 95, top	Courtesy of Forest History Society.
p. 95, bottom	Courtesy of Mississippi Forestry Commission.
p. 96, top	Courtesy of James E. Fickle.
p. 96, bottom	Courtesy of James E. Fickle.
p. 97	Courtesy of James E. Fickle.
p. 98, top	Courtesy of James E. Fickle.
p. 98, bottom	Courtesy of James E. Fickle.
p. 99	Photograph courtesy of Susan Jackson Keig. In Thomas D. Clark, *The Greening of the South: The Recovery of Land and Forest* (Lexington: University Press of Kentucky, 1984).
p. 100, left	Courtesy of Forest History Society.
p. 100, right	Photograph from Ruby Miller and John Maddocks Collections in *Journal of Forest History*, vol. 20, no. 2 (April 1976), 91.
p. 101, top	Courtesy of the Weston family.
p. 101, center	Courtesy of John Guthrie.
p. 101, bottom	Courtesy of Special Collections Department, Mitchell Memorial Library, Mississippi State University.
p. 102, top	Courtesy of Special Collections Department, Mitchell Memorial Library, Mississippi State University.
p. 102, bottom left	Photograph in *Reveille*, Vol 68 (1973), 352. Copy in Special Collections Department, Mitchell Memorial Library, Mississippi State University.
P. 102, bottom right	Courtesy of Polly Anderson.
p. 103, top	Courtesy of Mrs. Dorothy Martin, Jr.
p. 103, center	Photograph in *Mississippi Forests* (Jackson: Mississippi Forestry Commission, 1968), 3.
p. 103, bottom	Courtesy of James Elledge.
p. 104, top	Courtesy of McCain Library and Archives, University of Southern Mississippi.
p. 104, bottom	Courtesy of Mississippi Forestry Commission.
p. 105, top	Courtesy of Mississippi Forestry Commission.
p. 105, bottom	Robert S. Maxwell and Robert D. Baker, *Sawdust Empire* (College Station: Texas A&M University Press, 1983), 179.
p. 106, top left	Courtesy of Mississippi Forestry Commission.
p. 106, top right	Courtesy of Mississippi Forestry Commission.
p. 106, bottom	Courtesy of Mississippi Forestry Commission.
p. 107	Photograph by Bluford W. Muir. Courtesy of U.S. Forest Service, Jackson, Mississippi.
p. 108, top	Courtesy of Arthur W. Nelson, Jr.
p. 108, bottom	Courtesy of Forest History Society.
p. 109, top	Courtesy of Mississippi Forestry Commission.
p. 109, bottom	Courtesy of John Guthrie.
p. 110, top	Courtesy of Mississippi Forestry Commission.

p. 110, bottom	Courtesy of Forest History Society.	p. 123	Courtesy of Glen Ray Harris.
p. 111	Courtesy of Mississippi Forestry Commission.	p. 124, top	Photograph by E. Richard Toole. Courtesy of U.S. Forest Service, Center for Bottomland Hardwoods Research.
p. 112, top	Courtesy of Louisiana Department of Agriculture and Forestry.	p. 124, center	Photograph by W. N. Darwin. Courtesy of U.S. Forest Service, Center for Bottomland Hardwoods Research.
p. 112, bottom	Photograph in *The South's Fourth Forest: Alternatives for the Future*, United States Department of Agriculture, Forest Service, Forest Resource Report No. 24 (Washington, 1988), 45.	p. 124, bottom	Photograph by R. M. Krinard. Courtesy of U.S. Forest Service, Center for Bottomland Hardwoods Research.
p. 113	Courtesy of Louisiana State University Department of Archives and Manuscripts.	p. 125, top	Courtesy of Mississippi Forestry Commission.
p. 114, top	Courtesy of John Guthrie.	p. 125, center	Photograph in *Tree Talk*, vol. 9, no. 1 (fall 1987), 15.
p. 114, bottom	Courtesy of John Guthrie.	p. 125, bottom	Courtesy of U.S. Forest Service, Jackson, Mississippi.
p. 115, top	Courtesy of Mississippi Forestry Commission.	p. 126, top	Courtesy of Forest History Society.
p. 115, bottom	Courtesy of Mississippi Forestry Commission.	p. 126, center	Courtesy of Forest History Society.
p. 116, top	Courtesy of Mississippi Forestry Commission.	p. 126, bottom	Courtesy of U.S. Forest Service, Jackson, Mississippi.
p. 116, bottom	Courtesy of Mississippi Forestry Commission.	p. 127, top	Courtesy of William T. Smith, Piave, Mississippi.
p. 117, top	Courtesy of Lauren Rogers Museum of Art Library, Laurel, Mississippi.	p. 127, center	Courtesy of U.S. Forest Service, Laurel, Mississippi.
p. 117, bottom	Courtesy of Lauren Rogers Museum of Art Library, Laurel, Mississippi.	p. 127, bottom	Courtesy of U.S. Forest Service, Jackson, Mississippi.
p. 118, top	Courtesy of Lauren Rogers Museum of Art Library, Laurel, Mississippi.	p. 128, top	Courtesy of U.S. Forest Service, Jackson, Mississippi.
p. 118, bottom	Photograph by Bluford W. Muir. Courtesy of U.S. Forest Service, Jackson, Mississippi.	p. 128, bottom	Courtesy of U.S. Forest Service, Jackson, Mississippi.
p. 119, top	Courtesy of East Texas Research Center, Ralph W. Steen Library, Stephen F. Austin State University.	p. 129, top	Courtesy of Mississippi Department of Archives and History, Jackson, Mississippi.
p. 119, bottom	Photograph by W. H. Marin. Courtesy of U.S. Forest Service, Jackson, Mississippi.	p. 129, bottom	Courtesy of U.S. Forest Service, Laurel, Mississippi.
p. 120, top	Courtesy of Mississippi Forestry Commission.	p. 130	Courtesy of U.S. Forest Service, Jackson, Mississippi.
p. 120, bottom	Photograph by W. H. Marin. Courtesy of U.S. Forest Service, Jackson, Mississippi.	p. 131, top	Courtesy of McCain Library and Archives, University of Southern Mississippi.
p. 121, top	Cooper Postcard Collection. Courtesy of Mississippi Department of Archives and History, Jackson, Mississippi.	p. 131, bottom	Courtesy of Mississippi Forestry Commission.
p. 121, bottom	Courtesy of Mississippi Forestry Commission.	p. 132, top	Photograph in *The Yazoo–Little Tallahatchie Flood Prevention Project: A History of the Forest Service's Role* (U.S. Department of Agriculture, Forest Service, Southern Region, Forestry Report R8-FR8, 1988), 15.
p. 122, top	Photograph courtesy of Weyerhaeuser Company. In Thomas D. Clark, *The Greening of the South: The Recovery of Land and Forest* (Lexington: University Press of Kentucky, 1984).	p. 132, bottom	Photograph in *The Yazoo–Little Tallahatchie Flood Prevention Project: A History of the Forest Service's Role* (U.S. Department of Agriculture, Forest Service, Southern Region, Forestry Report R8-FR8, 1988), 17.
p. 122, bottom	Courtesy of Mississippi Forestry Commission.		

p. 133, top	Photograph in *The Forest Returns to the Yazoo* (Atlanta: U.S. Forest Service, Southern Region, 1960), 17.
p. 133, center	Photograph in *The Forest Returns to the Yazoo* (Atlanta: U.S. Forest Service, Southern Region, 1960), 17.
p. 133, bottom	U.S. Forest Service photograph by Todd. Courtesy of Mississippi Forestry Commission.
p. 134, top	Courtesy of Mississippi Forestry Commission.
p. 134, bottom	U.S. Army Signal Corps photograph. Courtesy of Louisiana State University Department of Archives and Manuscripts.
p. 135, top	U.S. Army Signal Corps photograph. Courtesy of Louisiana State University Department of Archives and Manuscripts.
p. 135, bottom left	Photograph in Carroll Brinson, *More Than a Good Businessman: The Story of Warren A. Hood* (Jackson, MS: Oakdale Press, 1987), 28.
p. 135, bottom right	Photograph in *Mississippi Forests* (Jackson: Mississippi Forestry Commission, 1968), 3.
p. 136, top	American Forest Products Industries, Inc., photograph. Courtesy of Forest History Society.
p. 136, center	U.S. Forest Service photograph in Robert S. Maxwell and Robert D. Baker, *Sawdust Empire* (College Station: Texas A&M University Press, 1983), 205.
p. 136, bottom	Courtesy of Forest History Society.
p. 137, top	Photograph by Bluford W. Muir. Courtesy of U.S. Forest Service, Jackson, Mississippi.
p. 137, center	Photograph by Bluford W. Muir. Courtesy of U.S. Forest Service, Jackson, Mississippi.
p. 137, bottom	Courtesy of Mississippi Forestry Commission.
p. 138, top	Photograph in *The South's Fourth Forest: Alternatives for the Future*, United States Department of Agriculture, Forest Service, Forest Resource Report No. 24 (Washington, 1988), 75.
p. 138, center left	Courtesy of Mississippi Forestry Commission.
p. 138, right	Photograph by Bluford W. Muir. Courtesy of U.S. Forest Service, Jackson, Mississippi.
p. 138, bottom left	Courtesy of Tommy Miller.
p. 139, top	Photograph in *Journal of Forestry*, vol. 69, no. 5 (May 1971), 285.
p. 139, center	Photograph in *Journal of Forestry*, vol. 69, no. 5 (May 1971), 287.
p. 139, bottom left	International Paper Company photograph. Courtesy of E. Jack Williams.
p. 139, bottom right	Courtesy of Anderson-Tully Lumber Company.
p. 140, top	Photograph by Tommy Miller. Courtesy of Tommy Miller.
p. 140, bottom	Photograph in *Tree Talk*, vol. 20, no. 2 (spring 1998), 23.
p. 141, top	Courtesy of James E. Fickle.
p. 141, bottom	Courtesy of Tommy Miller.
p. 142, top	Photograph in *The South's Fourth Forest: Alternatives for the Future*, United States Department of Agriculture, Forest Service, Forest Resource Report No. 24 (Washington, 1988), 70.
p. 142, bottom left	Photograph by Dr. Nathan Schiff. Courtesy of U.S. Forest Service, Stoneville, Mississippi.
p. 142, bottom right	Photograph by Charles "Bo" Sloan. Courtesy of U.S. Department of Agriculture, Wildlife Services, Stoneville, Mississippi.
p. 143, top left	Courtesy of James E. Fickle.
p. 143, top right	Courtesy of James E. Fickle.
p. 143, bottom	Courtesy of Crosby Arboretum.
p. 144, top	Courtesy of James E. Fickle.
p. 144, bottom	Courtesy of James E. Fickle.